COMPLETE
martial arts
GUIDE

COMPLETE martial arts GUIDE

Ray Pawlett, Roy Inman, Mark Pawlett,
Peter Warr and John Ritschel

Published by SILVERDALE BOOKS
An imprint of Bookmart Ltd
Registered number 2372865
Trading as Bookmart Ltd
Blaby Road
Wigston
Leicester LE18 4SE

© 2006 D&S Books Ltd

D&S Books Ltd
Kerswell,
Parkham Ash, Bideford
Devon, England
EX39 5PR

e-mail us at:- enquiries@d-sbooks.co.uk

This edition printed 2006

ISBN 10 – 1845094298
13 – 9781845094294

DS094. Complete Martial Arts Guide

Creative Director: Sarah King
Project Editor: Claire Bone
Photography: Colin Bowling/Paul Forrester
Designer: Debbie Fisher

Fonts: Avenir, Haettenschweiler

Material from this book previously appeared in The Karate Handbook, The Judo Handbook, The Tae Kwon Do Handbook, The Kung Fu Handbook, The Ju Jitsu Handbook and The Kickboxing Handbook.

Printed in Thailand

1 3 5 7 9 10 8 6 4 2

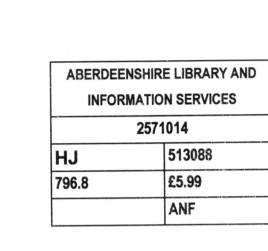

contents

introduction

Over the centuries, many forms of martial art have developed in different countries throughout the world. Complete Guide to Martial Arts looks at six of the most popular hard styles of martial arts and provides an overview of their backgrounds, philosophies and techniques.

Many people, when they think of martial arts, will automatically think of Bruce Lee, or perhaps the highly choreographed fight sequences in films such as "Crouching Tiger, Hidden Dragon" or "The Matrix". While some of the more advanced moves within each style may well be quite spectacular, the philosophy behind the martial arts are far removed from the aggression so often seen on screen .

Self-discipline, restraint, respect and courtesy are the cornerstones of these martial arts. The balance of mind, body and spirit is an important ethos, as well as increasing stamina, reducing stress and providing a focus for energy and this is what inspires millions of people around the world diligently to train in their chosen martial arts' styles.

Martial arts styles can also be explained as 'systems'. There is an input, a process and an output system involved. A suitable analogy for a martial arts' system would be 'the Cauldron', which is taken from the Chinese book of the I-Ching.

Imagine the ingredients of a cauldron with some of the many different aspects of martial arts. The cauldron is the martial artist and the fire below represents the spirit of the martial artist. When heat is applied to the cooking pot a transformation will take place. The ingredients will cook together to provide a nourishing meal. The pot will look the same from the outside, but important changes will have happened inside.

The true martial artist will add different elements of their style in a similar way. He or she will apply their own spirit in order to 'cook up' the ingredients. After a time the martial artist will be 'cooked', and an inner transformation will have taken place. This is not to say that you cannot keep adding ingredients, but it is a good idea to let the ones that you have in your pot start to cook first.

This is the key difference between a true martial arts' style and a sophisticated way of beating somebody up- the artist will be seeking this type of transformation. The transformations are an ongoing process - you cannot overcook this dish!

Hard and soft styles

Today you will find that the phrases 'hard' and 'soft' are used to describe categories of different martial arts styles. The general impression is that hard styles of martial art are very athletic and are therefore only suitable for the young and fit, whilst the soft styles are slow and therefore primarily for older people who want to focus on relaxation and stress reduction.

This is to look at the arts in an oversimplified way. In the East, the difference is not considered to be so clearcut. A true martial artist will need to have an

instinctive feel and understanding of what the hard and soft styles are and will need to respect both systems of working.

Another way of describing hard styles is 'external'. This is because importance is placed on muscular strength. Hard styles of martial arts will concentrate on strength training and the movements will generally be in straight and direct lines of force. Common examples and ones that we will look at in depth are Karate, Judo, Tae Kwon Do, some Kung Fu, Ju Jitsu and Kickboxing.

Soft styles are also referred to as 'internal' styles because of their emphasis on using energy (Chi or Ki) from within. Movements are always curved and never in straight lines. Examples of soft styles are Tai Chi, and Aikido.

The hard and soft styles can be compared to each other when imagining the common yin/yang symbols; opposites merge into each other and become a part of the same thing. This is also true of the hard and soft styles of martial arts on a large scale and a small scale.

Why different Styles?

All martial artists must have one final goal in mind: the raising of spirit. The varying different styles can be viewed as different pathways to the peak of the same mountain.

Some may ask the question why so many different pathways? As this is sure to cause confusion? Even within a single style of martial art, there are usually many different ways of executing the style. For example, within the karate style there are different versions, such as Shotokan, Koyokushinki and Wado Ru. The answer supplied by many masters is that simply choosing your correct pathway is half the effort towards climbing your individual mountain.

The different styles are not there to confuse and bewilder the beginner. The real reason for the manifold varieties of style is quite simple. We are all different people, so the style that we will prefer as individuals will therefore be different by necessity.

Some will have the right temperament for Ju Jitsu, one of the oldest of the Japanese martial arts, but if you cannot endure practicing such movements as strangleholds and joint locks, then maybe you should consider another style.

The popularity of Judo is partly because it appeals to such a wide audience. It is suitable for all ages and you don't have to be any more fit than your neighbour to start learning Judo; and continued practice will increase your strength, stamina and suppleness.

You may choose Tae Kwon Do the famous of the Korean martial arts. A fast and dynamic martial art it

will improve your suppleness and cardiovascular fitness.

It is Kung Fu that many people would associate with the dramatic fighting sequences seen in films. The Kung Fu student needs very little equipment to study the art and does not require a high level of fitness at the beginning. Continued practice will improve fitness and strength, but the student should not be dissuaded from studying the art if you do not consider yourself a highly fit person to begin with.

Kickboxing is the ultimate workout. It produces kick boxers who are strong, fast, fit and very conditioned. Kickboxing training gets you into top physical shape, toning your body by reducing body fat. That it also

teaches the art of self-defence is very appealing to a lot of people.

Another interesting aspect of martial arts is that they have usually been influenced by the history, folklore and customs of the country of origin. This is how martial arts' knowledge can also give you an insight into foreign cultures. Although there are many similarities between the styles, it is interesting to note the often subtle cultural differences. It is therefore up to the individual which path they take.

warm-up

neck warm-up
Repeat the exercises below ten to fifteen times.

1 Stand with your feet a shoulder-width apart. Relax, and move your chin gently forward, towards your chest.

2 Now bring your head back up and relax the stretch.

3 Look straight ahead and tilt the left side of your face towards your left shoulder.

4 Now release the tension and tilt your head to the right.

5 Turn your head so that you are looking left.

6 Release your stance and turn to the right.

shoulder warm-up

Much of karate is to do with blocks, strikes and punches from the arms. If your shoulders are as stiff as old pieces of wood, it is impossible for you to perform these actions smoothly.

shoulder exercise 1: rotations

This is a very simple exercise. If you have neck problems, it can be helpful because it can reduce tension in the trapezius muscles in the back of the neck.

1 Inhale as you raise your shoulders in an upward arc.

2 Exhale as you lower your shoulders in a downward arc.

3 Repeat in the other direction.

shoulder exercise 2: windmill

This exercise can be performed quickly or slowly. If you do it slowly, it is good to open the joint. Increasing the speed reduces the ability to open the joint, but helps to get the blood pumping around your shoulder area. To do the exercise, just swing your arm around in a circle. Try to perform a similar amount of exercise in both directions with each arm.

variation

For a more challenging exercise, swing one arm forwards and one arm backwards.

waist warm-up

In martial arts, the hips, waist and abdominal area are the core of your movement. In traditional Japanese shiatsu medicine, the hara (your abdominal region) is your energy centre. If your range of motion in this area is limited, then the whole way that you move your body will also be limited.

waist exercise 1: rotation

Try to keep your body held straight so that the movement is in your waist and not in your head bobbing up and down. One way of doing this is to focus your eyes on an object. If it looks like the object is moving, then ease off with the exercise until you are within a range of motion when you can keep your head still.

1 Start in a standing position. Put your hands on your kidneys.

2 Push forwards with your hands. Rotate your body to the left or right.

3 Repeat in the other direction.

Back view.

waist exercise 2: rotation

This exercise is fundamental to the way in which martial arts work. If you can use your waist area to create a rotation that transmits through your arm, you will have a powerful strike. Gradually slow down to a stop when you are ready to finish this waist exercise.

1 Start in a standing position. Turn your waist to the left and then to the right, keeping your arms relaxed.

2 As the momentum of your waist increases, your arms will swing out further. Do not throw your arms out.

legs warm-up

legs exercise 1

Repeat this exercise ten to fifteen times.

legs exercise 2

1 Stand with your feet together and place your hands on your knees.

2 Then push your knees forward.

legs exercise 3

1 Holding your right foot, pull your heel towards your bottom. Try to hold this position for twenty to thirty seconds.

2 Now do the same with your left leg.

If necessary, rest your hand against a wall in order to keep your balance.

1 Stand with your feet a shoulder-width apart and put your hands on your hips.

2 Now slowly bend your knees, keeping your body upright and your back straight. Slowly descend until your legs form a 90-degree angle.

When ascending to return to the starting position, make sure that your knees are slightly bent.

knees warm-up

If you have delicate knees, this exercise is probably best avoided as it is possible that it may aggravate the condition. If you feel any pain whatsoever during the exercise, you should either ease off or stop completely.

knee exercise 1: rotation

You will find that this exercise is excellent for loosening the hip joints and also for strengthening the thighs. When you have finished this exercise, repeat with the other leg.

1 Start by lifting your knee high in front of your body.

2 Draw a circle with your knee in one direction. Count the amount of circles that you do and perform the same number in the other direction.

knee exercise 2: rotation

In karate, you will be kicking. Your stance work also requires that your legs are strong and supple. These exercises can help.

1 Put your feet together, bend your knees and place your hands on your knees.

2 Rotate your knees, first in one direction and then in the other. Do not overdo the rotation, though.

ankles warm-up

Do not forget about your ankles! In stance work, your feet are your connection with the floor. If your ankles are stiff, then the vital connection between your body and the floor is reduced. It is also useful to have supple ankles for kicking.

ankle exercise 1: rotation

This exercise is shown being performed in the standing position, but you can also do it while sitting at a desk. Nobody will see you doing it, and it can have a grounding quality when used in this way.

1 Touch the floor with the ball of your foot. Make a rotation with your knee. This will work the ankle.

2 Try performing the rotation in both directions. Work with both legs.

ankle exercise 2: ankle stretch

Stretch your instep by placing the tops of your toes on the floor and gently pushing forwards.

meditation

I have discussed what they think the main differences are between training in the West and training in the East with many martial artists from Japan, Korea and China. One of the most common things mentioned is meditation.

In the West, we all too often do not make time for meditation, and therefore lose out on its benefits. Among the many benefits of meditation are a reduction in stress (thereby helping the immune system) and increased clarity of thought.

Now, clarity of thought is a pretty useful thing in karate. Imagine that you are trying to break something with your punch. Do you think that you can manage it if your mind is wandering? The same applies to kata and sparring. If you cannot focus your mind, you will sooner or later reach a point beyond which you cannot progress.

Meditation is like weight-lifting for the mind. In the beginning, sitting there trying to do and think nothing may feel odd, and even pointless until you have experienced the results.

If you can only manage to meditate for a few minutes a day, then so be it! You can work on it in the same way that you would on anything else, namely gradually. If you find meditation difficult in the beginning, this may indicate that it is what your mind and body need. Great fruits will be reaped!

There are many methods of meditation, including practising karate. We will now take a look at a very simple, but effective, meditation method called breathing into the hara.

breathing into the hara

Your hara is your energy centre. Focusing your breathing into that area is useful for calming your energy. You may find this technique especially useful if your daily routine forces you to train at night. It will help you to calm your body and mind and aids restful sleep.

1	Assume the kneeling position shown here, with your hands resting gently on your thighs. If this makes your knees feel uncomfortable, try sitting on cushions or cross-legged. The kneeling position gives you a firm base on which to support your back and keep it straight.
2	Close your eyes and listen to your breathing. Is it fast, slow, regular, irregular, deep or shallow? Do not judge, just notice.
3	Now turn your attention to the point where your hands are resting on your abdomen. When you breathe in and out, do your hands move?
4	Gently try to adjust your breathing rhythm so that your hands move outwards when you inhale and inwards when you exhale. You are now doing abdominal breathing, a popular technique in martial arts and yoga.
5	Carry on with the abdominal breathing for a few deep breaths. Feel the air going deep into your lungs. Imagine that you are breathing air down, into your abdomen.
6	After a few good, deep breaths to clear your lungs, breathe more gently. Try to make your breathing as smooth and deep as you can. This should be a very gentle stage of the meditation. Imagine that the point under your hands is becoming denser as you breathe into it.
7	Try to make your breathing silent, but deep. Continue visualising bringing energy into your hara.
8	When you have had enough, gently bring yourself out of the meditation. Shake your body about to bring it back to life again and to distribute the ki.

chapter one

karate

Karate is a Japanese martial art. It is practised by millions of people around the world of all ages, races and physical abilities. It is equally suitable for men and women as it relies on technique rather than pure physical strength.

Karate has developed in many different ways. It can be looked upon as an art form, a spiritual path, a sport, a self-defence system, a fitness routine or all of these things. Underneath this myriad of reflections lies the essence of karate.

Karate has its roots in the traditional ju jitsu of Japan, and specifically Okinawa, deep roots that have never been forgotten.

Karate emphasises strikes and blocks. The strikes and blocks can be made with many different parts of the body. One of the lessons of karate is how to use different parts of your body to attack or defend to the maximum advantage. The advanced karate student will also be able to employ lock, strangles and throws.

Respect and courtesy are integral parts of the teachings of karate. Karate students must learn respect for themselves, others and the world at large.

Karate has its philosophical roots in Zen Buddhism. The ways of Zen permeate through the whole of the strategy and framework of karate. It can be said that on many levels, the study of karate is the study of Zen Buddhism. Karate is therefore inherently peaceful, and the final opponent that one always meets before making any improvements is oneself.

Japan and Okinawa

Karate comes from Japan. To be more precise, what we know as karate actually originated in a small island near Japan called Okinawa. When trying to understand the history of karate, it is useful to have a good idea of where Okinawa is in relationship to Japan and China.

Okinawa is a small Japanese island measuring 10km (about 6 miles) wide by 110km (about 42 miles) long. It is the main island in the Ryuku group of islands that spans from China to Japan. It is nearly equidistant between China, Japan and Taiwan. During its history, it developed into an important resting spot and trading post between China, Japan, Taiwan, Thailand, Malaysia, Borneo and the Philippines. Indeed, the commercial importance of Okinawa's position was also seen as having strategic importance during World War II. It was the site of the famous battle for the 'Sugar Loaf' that lasted for ten days.

Knowing the position of Okinawa is important because it helps one to understand the different influences that combined to create karate.

Farming and fishing are the principal industries of Okinawa, although the biggest export by far must now be karate.

the history of karate

According to legend, a Buddhist monk named Bodidharma walked barefoot from India to China. When in China, he found a temple called Shaolin–Si ('small forest temple') and taught the monks Zen Buddhism. Part of his teaching was an exercise system that could be used to defend oneself. This is how the very famous shaolin style of kung fu is said to have evolved. Shaolin kung fu became the base upon which many of the Chinese martial arts were developed.

As we have seen, the island of Okinawa lies on an important trading route between China and Japan. The Okinawans had their own form of martial-arts training. The style of the martial art varied between the small towns on the island. (Do not forget how small the island is.) The variations tended to be along the lines of emphasising different movements rather than changing the actual movements themselves.

The martial style of Okinawa was known as te, or 'the empty hand'. The regional variations were collectively known as Okinawa–te.

Now, as history has often shown, if you are living on a small island on an important trading route, you are in a spot that is likely to be invaded. During the thirteenth century, the Japanese took over the island and then banned the carrying of weapons.

Then the influence of the Chinese styles of martial art made itself known. As the Chinese styles that were adopted were bare-hand forms of combat, the carrying of weapons was no longer a requirement.

An interesting legend about this time tells that much of the training was done at night, when the Japanese shogun was sleeping. It is said that the training clothes used were also sleeping clothes. Hence the birth of the karate suit, or gi.

This fighting style became known as tode, or 'the Chinese hand'. The Chinese character for tode can also be pronounced 'kara'. This was coupled with the original 'te' and so the word 'karate' was invented. The original meaning of the word 'karate' was thus 'the Chinese hand'.

Later, the karate master Gichin Funakoshi adopted the alternative meaning of the Chinese character kara, which is 'empty', and added the word 'do' to the name. The word 'do' means 'path' or 'way'. The name 'karate do' had been born, meaning 'the way of the empty hand'.

The idea of 'do' was not new. If you read Buddhist writings from times long predating Funakoshi, it is clear that the concept had always been there. The 'way' that is implied is a spiritual path towards enlightenment.

Nearly every sport, science, martial art or art form has a person in its history who is said to have brought it to the world's attention and revolutionised it. In karate, we have Gichin Funakoshi.

Gichin Funakoshi was an Okinawan who was born in 1868 and died in 1957. He was taught martial arts in the beginning by many of the most notable Okinawan martial artists, including Azato and Itosu.

Gichin Funakoshi, like many other martial artists, was not a particularly strong child. When of primary-school age, Master Azato taught him the ways of the martial arts and improved his strength. Funakoshi was also an intelligent child who became well read in many of the classics of Chinese and Japanese knowledge.

In 1917, Funakoshi travelled from Okinawa to Kyoto to give his first martial-arts demonstration at the request of the Japanese Ministry for Education. A few years later, in 1921, he gave another demonstration to Crown Prince Hirohito at Shuri Castle. The crown prince was highly impressed with the display.

In 1922, Dr Jigoro Kano (the founder of judo) invited Funakoshi to teach karate at the Kodokan Dojo, a famous place of martial-arts learning at the time. This allowed Funakoshi to become established in Japan and his karate to get a foothold in the country.

Eventually, Funakoshi was able to afford his own dojo, or training hall. Funakoshi had the nickname Shoto, meaning 'waving pines'. The Japanese word for hall is 'kan'. The two words were put together, so that people were said to train at Shotokan, or 'Shoto's hall'. The word 'shotokan' became synonymous with his training style and was adopted as the name for that style of karate.

While it is true that Funakoshi was the originator of the shotokan style, it was, however, his son, Yoshitaka Funakoshi, who developed it into the form that we know today. It seems that the father developed the system and the son understood how to teach the system and bring it to the people.

In 1922, Hironori Ohtsuka (1892–1982) began studying karate with Funakoshi. He had already had a long training in ju jitsu before meeting Funakoshi. In 1939, he started his own style and called it 'wado–ryu'. 'Wado ryu' translates as 'the way of harmony'. In wado–ryu, to show aggression is discouraged. For this reason, it is sometimes translated as 'the peaceful way'.

Wado–ryu combines the basic movements of ju jitsu with techniques of evasion, putting a strong emphasis on softness of movement.

Another karate style that originated in Okinawa was goju–ryu. The style was developed by Kanryo Higaonna (1853–1915), who opened a school on the island. The core of his teaching stems from eight forms that he bought from China. His top student, Chojun Miyagi (1888–1953), founded the goju–ryu style in 1930. 'Goju–ryu' means 'hard–soft way'. The emphasis in goju–ryu is upon soft, circular blocking techniques, with a strong counter-attack being quickly delivered.

Shito–ryu was founded in 1928 by Kenwa Mabuni (1889–1952), and was directly influenced by the Okinawan styles. The name 'shito' is constructed from the names of Mabuni's teachers, Ankoh Itosu and Kanryo Higaonna. The style uses a large number of kata (around fifty) and emphasises power in the execution of the techniques.

As you can see from the dates given for these styles, they have all been developed relatively recently. In one way or another, most of the modern karate styles can be traced back to Gichin Funakoshi. For this reason, he is sometimes called 'the grandfather of karate'. His memorial bears the phrase 'There is no first attack in karate', emphasising his peaceful nature.

The symbol of the wado–ryu school of karate.

Karate continues to develop as it did in the days of Funakoshi. Nowadays, there are many different styles, so I apologise if I have missed out yours! Each style has its own emphasis and tactical method. Nevertheless, one thing can be said about all of the styles: the goal is the same, namely that of spiritual peace and harmony. A common phrase used to describe the styles is that they are all 'paths up the same mountain'.

In 1964, an attempt was made to formulate a set of rules that would encompass all of the styles so that competitions could be held between the styles by the Federation of All Japan Karate–do Organisation (FAJKO). In 1970, the first 'all-styles' karate world championships were held in Tokyo. At the same time, a meeting was held and the World Union of Karate–do Organisations was formed.

The diversity of styles makes it impossible for us to look at them all in this book. Instead, we shall look at many of the techniques that are common to all styles, although the execution may vary. We shall also look at some of the kata from the shotokan style.

is karate for me?

Is karate suitable for you? Well, in short, if you want to do it: yes. The first and most important thing that a karateka must have is the desire to do it. Obviously, this desire will vary from person to person.

You may find that you want to train a lot and eventually become a black belt. Or you may find that a little is enough. In martial arts, the rule is that the more you put into it, the more you get out of it.

So what age range suits karate? Remember when we discussed Gichin Funakoshi? He started his karate training at primary-school age, the youngest age that children should take up karate. Karate can be an ideal sport for children as it can teach them discipline and self-confidence, backed up by fitness training.

If you are thinking of taking a child to a karate class, speak to the sensei. If the sensei considers your child mature enough for the dojo, then give it a go. Ensure that the sensei understands that children's bodies have not finished growing and that some of the harder stretches and conditioning exercises should therefore be left until they are older. A school will usually also wait for a while before teaching them some of the more dangerous attacking techniques.

No matter what your age, you can have a go at learning karate. If you are worried about your fitness, talk to the sensei and consult your doctor. There are very few medical complaints that will completely exclude you from karate if you have the desire to train, and if you, your sensei and your doctor can together devise a training plan, you should be alright. The more mature student usually finds the concepts of karate easy to grasp, and a karate club can be a great place to meet new friends, too!

There is no reason why men should be better at karate than women. Although some men occasionally try to dominate a sparring session if they are physically stronger than a woman, a sensei will always stop this. In my experience, it is usually the man who loses out if he tries that trick!

what do I need?

When you first enter the dojo or training hall, most teachers will allow you to train in tracksuit bottoms and a T-shirt. Karate is usually performed barefoot, which saves on the cost of footwear!

1	gum shield	A gum shield costs a lot less than getting your teeth fixed. Buy one that won't slip out of your mouth.
2	groin protector	I don't need to say much about why a groin protector is advisable! A proper martial-arts groin protector will protect you better than a 'cricket-box' type. The further it covers your abdominal region without limiting your movement, the better.
3	bust protector	Women will need a bust protector.

If you then decide that karate is for you, you will be expected to buy a gi. The gi is the traditional outfit worn for training in many martial arts. Karate gis tend to be made from lighter material than judo gis because they are less likely to be torn. The cost of a basic gi usually starts at around £15.

Karate clothes have suffered the same fate as other clothing items: they start low in price, but can become very expensive. There is usually no practical reason why an expensive gi should be better than a cheaper one.

After a while, your sensei will start to teach you kumite, or sparring. If you are to practise free sparring, it is wise to invest in protective equipment. Try to buy the best that you can afford as it will work better and last longer. You can buy all manner of body armour and headgear, some of which are not used by certain karate associations. Your sensei will advise you if you need to buy it. If it is essential, the club will usually have enough supplies.

There are some items that you will need to buy, as outlined in the box below left.

belts and grades

When you go to your first karate class, you will see the karate students arranged in neat lines. The ones at the front will probably have black belts, the ones at the back, white belts, while the ones in the middle will be wearing belts of a variety of colours. The colours of the belts are not a fashion statement. They tell you the level of training that the karateka has reached through his or her gradings.

The colour of the belts follows a sequence that starts with a white belt and finishes with a black belt. The colours of the belts in between tell you what grade the intermediate karateka has attained.

Each of the belts has to be won in an examination called a grading. This idea was invented by Jigoro Kano, the founder of judo. If you remember your karate history, you'll know that Gichin Funakoshi, the 'grandfather of karate', was acquainted with Jigoro Kano. It is therefore not surprising that he adopted the practice, which instantly identifies the more advanced students.

There is a story that after World War II, when Japan was a very poor country, karatekas would dye their belts progressively darker colours until they became black belts.

Nowadays, the many different schools of karate have different colours for their belts. It is important to know the grading system of the school that you are in. In some schools, a blue belt denotes quite an advanced student, for example, while in others, the blue belt is a beginner's belt. In the box below, you will see the traditional colours of the belts, ranging from white to black, in shotokan karate.

There are usually also intermediate grades between the belts, which are denoted by a stripe on the belt.

The word 'kyu' means grades away from the black belt (dan). For example, 8th kyu means that the karateka has eight more full gradings to achieve before he or she wins the coveted black belt.

When you reach black-belt level, it does not stop there! Many say that it has just started! There are various levels of black belt, called 'dan grades'. The higher the number, the higher the grade, which is denoted by a stripe on the end of the black belt.

In your grading, you will be required to show the latest kata that you have been learning and possibly some previous ones. Your basic movements, or kihon, will be inspected, and you will have to do some kumite, or sparring.

The mixture and type of each kata, kumite and kihon will vary, depending on your grade. For example, the beginner is not expected to show any kumite. A black belt, by contrast, will have to show fixed-pattern kumite and free sparring with other black belts.

level	grade	
beginner		white belt
10th kyu		blue belt
9th kyu		red belt
8th kyu		orange belt
7th kyu		orange belt with yellow stripes
6th kyu		yellow belt
5th kyu		green belt
4th kyu		purple belt
3rd kyu		brown belt
2nd kyu		brown belt with white stripes
1st kyu		brown belt with red stripes
1st dan		black belt

the karate class

So much for the theory. Without the practice, it amounts to nothing more than intellectual play. So, you have decided to try karate. What next?

Well, you have two options. You could either try to learn from books like this one and take years to master the techniques in a very limited manner, or you could short-circuit that idea and join a class.

Hopefully, you will opt for the 'join a class' option. We will take a look at ways of determining what sort of class you are joining later, but for now, let's consider what happens when you go to a class.

It is normally best to contact the sensei, or teacher, before you go to a class. Although many teachers do not demand that you do this, it gives them a chance to meet you for a few minutes before the class starts. The sensei will normally want to talk to you about any specific needs (medical or non-medical) that you may have. It also gives you the opportunity to get to know your teacher.

What happens next depends on the teacher. Some teachers will ask you to watch for a while so that you can decide whether or not to take the plunge. It is more common these days for the new karate student (karateka) to join in with the beginners. Sometimes a higher-graded student will teach you the basics, such as dojo courtesy.

The class will always start with warm-up exercises of some description. Then the class will usually consist of a mixture of basics (kihon), patterns (kata) and sparring (kumite). The ratio of these will usually vary, depending on the club and what the sensei wants to work on in that lesson. Another addition that will normally be inserted at various times during the class is stretching exercises.

We will analyse the three physical training areas, kihon, kata and kumite, throughout this chapter.

dojo etiquette

Whenever you enter or leave a karate dojo, you should always make a bow, or 'rei' (pronounced 'ray'). It matters not whether it is a purpose-built dojo or the local village hall: for the purposes of a karate lesson, they are the same. Even if you are just leaving to visit the bathroom, you should always rei on the way out and on the way back in.

At the beginning and end of your class, you will perform either the standing rei or the kneeling rei. When the sensei tells you to split up into couples for kumite, you should rei to the sensei before breaking away from the group.

The bow, or 'rei', is one of the ways in which a karateka shows respect.

You should find your partner quickly and greet him or her with a rei. Before training with your partner, you should rei, and when you have finished training with your partner, you should rei. If you are going to train with another partner, you should do the same again.

So what is all of this bowing for? Many non-martial artists guess that it is similar to shaking hands. This notion probably comes from the habit that Japanese people have of bowing to each other rather than shaking hands. Other people sometimes say that it is kowtowing to the sensei's ego. Both reasons are completely and emphatically wrong!

The rei is a sign of respect. When you enter or leave the dojo, it is a sign that you have respect for the dojo. When you bow to the sensei, you are not bowing to show subservience to the person standing in front of you. You are bowing to show respect for that person, for what he or she has done in the pursuit of karate knowledge and for all that has gone before him or her.

If you bow to the teachers of the past, you are bowing to the work that they have done and to that which was done before and after them.

When you bow to your training partner, you are showing your partner respect and gratitude for the chance to train with him or her, whoever he or she may be.

With the rei, you should feel a sense of openness and respect. It is nothing at all to do with your ego or that of the person to whom you are bowing. If you subtract the element of respect from martial arts, you are removing one of the most valuable lessons that they have to teach, both to individuals and to the world at large.

There are two sorts of rei that are commonly used in karate, the kneeling rei and the standing rei. Both are very important, so we shall now look at each in turn.

the kneeling rei

The kneeling rei is the most formal version of the rei. It is used at the beginning and end of the class and when bowing to the masters of the past.

1 Start in the attention stance.

2 Move into the ready stance.

3 Bend your right knee. Look ahead.

4 Bend your left knee and kneel down.

5 Drop your weight onto your heels.

6 Place your hands on the floor, thumbs and forefingers touching. Look ahead.

7 Lower your head.

8 Place your right hand on your right thigh.

9 Place your left hand on your left thigh.

To come out of the position, follow the instructions in reverse order. Note that you will always start by putting your left knee on the floor first. This is because the samurai, who wore their swords on the left, used exactly the same bow. Placing the left knee on the floor first got the weapon out of the way, enabling them to bow.

the standing rei

The standing rei is the rei that is used the most frequently. It is also the one that is performed incorrectly the most often! The standing rei is always performed when you need to show courtesy and respect, such as when approaching a new training partner or when leaving or entering the dojo.

1 Start in the ready stance.

2 Place your heels together in the attention stance.

3 Bend forward from the waist, looking ahead.

stances and stepping

One of the most important aspects of martial-arts training, whether it is in karate or any other style, is footwork. If your footwork is not good, then you need to work on it. No successful martial artist ever considered footwork to be unimportant.

Imagine, for a moment, a cannon on board a ship or defending the ramparts of a castle. When a cannonball is fired, there is a reaction from the explosion in the gunpowder. This reaction causes the cannonball to shoot out, but also forces the cannon to move backwards if it is not securely fixed into place.

This is one of the principles upon which karate stances are based. If you fire out your fist like a cannonball, you have released a good punch. But if your feet slip back, some energy is wasted. This is not good because part of what you are trying to achieve in karate is focusing all of your energy into a single point.

Now imagine that you actually hit something. This time, the reaction will be even stronger because the impact reflects backwards through your body as a reaction force. If the reaction force knocks you off balance or throws you back, you will probably be in worse trouble than you were before the punch!

The solution to this is to use a good, strong stance ('dachi' in Japanese) that can withstand the impact of the reaction to your techniques. The stances in karate are similar to those in most martial arts. For example, the front stance in karate is also used in other Japanese arts, such as judo and aikido. Chinese and Korean styles tend towards slightly shorter stances for reasons of their own, although this is not a hard-and-fast rule.

The next thing to be concerned with after your stance is how to move in that stance. If you are rooted to the spot, you will not be much of a martial artist! When stepping, the physics are designed to try to maintain the integrity of the stance. This means that you should be well balanced when making transitions between your stances.

Your stepping and stances are also the key to your distancing. If you are good with your footwork, it is possible to throw a person off balance just by stepping towards them in the correct way. Clearly, correct footwork is an aspect of the art that will be refined throughout your progress in karate. How you understand your footwork in a year's time should be different to your current comprehension.

1	Stand to attention, with your arms by your sides.
2	Cross your forearms.
3	Step forward with your right foot as you uncross your arms.

natural stance: hachiji dachi

The natural stance is the one that you use at the beginning of all of the katas and other formal exercises. The stance is sometimes called the 'yoi' stance for that reason.

Your body should be straight and well aligned. This shows that you have strong spirit. Stay alert when in the stance. If you allow your mind to drift when in the stance before performing your kata at a grading, for example, your instructor will notice. You will have made your first mistake before actually doing anything. Karate is as much about your state of mind as your body!

The natural stance is a neutral stance that is neither aggressive nor retreating. Your feet should be a hip-width apart.

The instructions to the left tell you how to get into the natural stance from the attention stance (heisoku dachi).

front stance: zenkutsu dachi

The front stance is a strong attacking stance that can also be used for blocks. The power of the stance is in pushing your energy and strength forwards, hence its obvious application for attacking. It can also be used to make a retreat. If you are in a situation where you need to retreat, but also display strength, you can step backwards in the front stance.

Your weight should be split approximately 70/30 between your legs, with 70 per cent on your front leg. The stance should be the width of your shoulders and one-and-a-half shoulder-widths in length. Your front leg should be bent at the knee and your back leg should be straight. Your hips should face forwards. Both feet should stay flat on the floor. Your rear foot should be at an angle of around 45 degrees.

This is probably the most common stance in karate. Try to programme your body so that you automatically step into it correctly.

Side view.

stepping in the front stance

1 Start in the natural stance (hachiji dachi).

2 Move your right leg forward and bend your knee. As you push forward from your left heel, allow your left foot to turn through an angle. Keep your right leg bent as you bring your left foot close to your right. At this moment, your weight should stay on your right leg. Try to keep your balance so that you do not wobble.

3 Step forward with your left foot into the next front stance.

To continue stepping, just follow this outlined sequence.

If you want to step backwards in the back stance, the procedure is exactly the same. Just follow the instructions given in reverse.

back stance: kokutsu dachi

As you can probably work out from your newly gleaned knowledge of the front stance, the back stance is primarily a defensive stance that can also be used for attacking.

In this stance, the weight split is still 70/30, but in reverse. Your back leg carries most of the weight. Your heels should be in line with each other. Again, the front foot is straight and the back foot is positioned at an angle.

This stance can be quite demanding for the standing leg because all of the muscles are compressed in that leg. As you start to tire, be careful that you do not lean forwards and put too much weight on your front leg or allow your knee to collapse. Remember your karate spirit! After training, your muscles will become accustomed to the stance and it will not feel difficult.

getting into the back stance

Follow the steps illustrated here to get into the back stance.

1 Start in the attention stance.

2 Turn your right foot to an angle of 45 degrees and move your left leg forwards.

3 Lower your weight onto your right leg and place your left heel on the floor.

straddle-leg stance: kiba dachi

The straddle-leg stance is sometimes called the horse or horse-riding stance. The idea is that you should look like you are riding a horse, which doesn't just mean having your legs apart. In horse riding, if you are on the flat, it is good to keep your back straight. And in this stance, it is essential that you keep your back straight.

The inner edges of your feet should be parallel and about two shoulder-widths apart. You need to sink down on to your knees, so your knees will be turned outwards slightly. Your weight should be equally distributed between your feet.

This stance is very useful for sideways attacks, such as the side-snapping kick. It can also be used as a stable base for a front attack if you want to deliver a powerful punch.

The straddle-leg stance can be very difficult for beginners because it is demanding on the muscles. Try standing in the posture for a few minutes a day to build up your strength.

cat stance: neko ashi dachi

The cat stance is so called because it is said to resemble the way that a cat steps. A cat will touch the floor with its foot before putting weight on it. In the cat stance, all of the weight is on the rear, standing leg, while the ball of the leading foot gently touches the floor.

It is a difficult stance to hold, but has a certain kind of elegance. For this reason, it is not included in most of the katas that a beginner will be expected to perform. However, you may be asked to show that you know the stance, so do not disregard it, even if you are a beginner.

The main usage for this stance is when you suddenly need to move your body backwards in a defensive posture. If you step back into the cat stance, your front leg is in an ideal position to deliver a front kick.

It is not usually a stance that is used for stepping in kata or kumite, although some clubs may encourage stepping in the cat stance to train the legs.

The cat stance is usually used as a defensive or retreating stance.

basic techniques

As with any skill or art form, there are certain basic techniques that you must understand before you learn the intricacies. With karate, they are the hand and foot techniques.

Generally speaking, these techniques are used either to strike or to evade a strike. When your understanding becomes deeper, you will begin to see that blocks can be used as strikes and vice versa. Some of the basic techniques also have applications as locks and throws.

For now, we will look at a single application for each technique. Always try to think of new applications for your techniques, though. This will help you to make your karate your own and also to learn very effectively.

If you want to improve your karate, work on your basic techniques. It is of little use knowing many different kata, but still not being able to punch your way out of a paper bag! If your technique is good, you can apply it to your kata, your sparring and everything else. Basic techniques are the building blocks of karate.

Improving one technique will have a positive effect on all of your other techniques. So start by learning one technique at a time, such as the lower block.

Practise the lower block, or whichever technique you have chosen to focus on, at home for five to ten minutes each day. Keep working on the same movement for six to eight weeks before moving on to the next one, for example, the punch.

straight punch: choku zuki

The straight punch is the basic building block of many of the other punches. It is fairly fast, and has the power to stop an opponent. It is versatile, and can be used on any target.

The most difficult parts of this punch are timing, or co-ordinating the left hand with the right hand (both should move at the same speed), and achieving the twist at the end of the punch. Because it is so fundamental to the karate style, it should always be practised.

The punch is shown being performed in the horse-riding stance. If it were done in the front stance, it would become another punch. It could also be executed in the back stance

The straight-punch application.

1	Contact area	two front knuckles
2	Range	medium to long
3	Target area	anywhere!
4	Power	strong
5	Speed	medium to fast
6	Difficulty level	easy
7	Suitability for sparring	good

Try practising the movement slowly to learn how to co-ordinate your hands, and gradually build up the speed. The more advanced karateka can perform dynamic tensioning.

1 Start in the horse-riding stance, with your left fist held out, and your right fist by your belt.

2 Pull your left elbow back as you start to push forward with your right fist.

3 Continue moving your elbow and fist. Both fists should stop moving at the same time, and that is when your wrist twists.

stepping punch: oi zuki

If you step forward into the front stance while executing a straight punch, you will have performed a stepping punch. This can be used when you need to get nearer to an opponent in order to hit him or her.

It is very a powerful punch because it concentrates the whole of your body weight into a very small striking area. It is not as fast as the choku zuki (straight) punch because you need to step to perform the punch.

As with all punches, timing is the key to maximising its power!

1	Contact area	two front knuckles
2	Range	long
3	Target area	frequently mid-section, but can be used anywhere
4	Power	very strong: it has the weight of your body behind it
5	Speed	medium
6	Difficulty level	easy, but requires co-ordination of the arms and legs
7	Suitability for sparring	good

Stepping-punch application.

1 Start in the left front stance, with your left arm held in the position for a low block.

2 Raise your left arm as you step up.

3 Step forward with your right leg into the right front stance.

4 Twist your body and pull back your left arm as you punch with your right fist.

striking

As well as punching techniques, karate has a wide variety of striking (uchi) techniques. Most of these can double up as blocking techniques. We will examine some of them here. The aim in striking is to use one of your contact areas to attack an opponent's strike area. Many of the striking techniques come more from the realm of unarmed combat than competition. A high-powered knife-hand strike to the neck, for example, can easily result in permanent injury. These techniques are, however, a valuable part of karate, and are vital ingredients of the karate spirit. In classes, they are studied in either kata or one-step sparring.

Outside-knife-hand-strike application.

outside knife-hand strike: soto shuto uchi

Some techniques in karate are just too dangerous for free sparring. The knife-hand techniques usually fall into this category. In sparring, as in anything else, it is possible to make mistakes, and a bad mistake with a knife-hand can result in serious injury.

The technique uses the edge of the hand and lends itself to attacking the sides of the body. The momentum comes from a circular motion that starts either just behind your head or near to your ear.

The technique can be performed as a stepping or a standing technique in any of the stances.

1	Contact area	the edge of the hand, on the side of the little finger
2	Range	medium to long
3	Target area	sides of the body, usually the neck or temple
4	Power	high
5	Speed	medium–fast
6	Difficulty level	easy
7	Suitability for sparring	not suitable for free sparring

1 Start by assuming the lower block position.

2 Now extend your left hand and raise your right hand.

3 Snap the technique into the finishing position as your left fist twists. Your right palm will be facing upwards.

ridge hand: haito uchi

The ridge-hand technique uses the opposite side of the hand to the knife-hand technique. When you use this technique, ensure that you keep your thumb well out of the way. If you do not, you may cause yourself a painful injury, even if you are only hitting a bag.

If you are facing your opponent, the attack areas will be the neck and temples. If you are sideways on to your opponent, the bridge of the nose is a good target area.

This is a very powerful technique that is frequently used for breaking wood.

Ridge-hand application.

1	Contact area	the edge of the hand, by the thumb
2	Range	medium to long
3	Target area	the sides of the body, usually the neck or temple
4	Power	high
5	Speed	medium–fast
6	Difficulty level	easy
7	Suitability for sparring	unsuitable for free sparring

ridge-hand strike from the ready stance

1 Start by assuming the lower block position.

2 Extend your left hand.

3 Pull back your left arm as your right arm snaps into position.

inside ridge hand

The technique shown here is for the outside ridge hand. As with the outside knife-hand strike, it is possible to use it as an inside technique.

blocking

It is possible to argue that blocking (uke) is a more important skill than attacking in martial arts. If you were able to evade or block every one of your opponent's attacks, then you would have successfully defended yourself. I do not think that any martial-art style uses this as its tactical philosophy, but it is a useful concept for underlining the importance of blocking.

The ultimate way of blocking an attack is simply not to be where the attack is. This can be done by side-steps and evasions. However, it may be that you need to get close to your opponent to counterattack, as when sparring, or that your opponent's attack cannot be neutralised by evasion and side-stepping.

In this situation, you will need to find a way of deflecting the attack. This is usually done with the forearm, although it is possible to use other parts of the body, such as the knee or elbow, to block an attack.

When learning blocking, think about what you will do after you have performed the block. This should always be to try to set up your opponent for your counterattack.

Blocks can be made to the high area (jodan), middle area (chudan) or low area (gedan). Taking these three body areas and other considerations into account, there is a wide range of blocks available to the karateka. We shall now examine some of them.

downward block: gedan barai

The downward block is probably the most basic karate technique. It is absolutely intrinsic to the way that karate works. For this reason, it is usually taught to karateka very early in their training, and yet is still included in more advanced kata.

This block uses the bottom of the fist or the outer forearm to strike the opponent's attack and knock it out of the way. You will usually see this block being performed in the front stance. It can also be done in any of the other stances.

A typical application for this block would be to defend against a lower front kick, as shown below left. Do not get stuck on this idea, though. What is to stop you from using exactly the same technique as a lower hammer-fist strike to the opponent's inside leg or groin?

When blocking, do not try to hit your opponent's fist or foot as it is all too easy to miss that target. It is better to use the block against your opponent's forearm or lower leg.

The downward block in action.

This block can also be used as a strike.

upward block: age uke

The second of the basic karate blocks is the upper block, or age uke. While the downward block protects the lower-groin area, this block protects the upper-head area.

It can be used to protect yourself against a kick or punch coming towards your face, as shown below.

A more advanced way of performing this block is to use it as an entangled-arm lock. In this sequence, the attacker comes towards you and you use the arm that would normally be the reaction arm to deflect the attack. You then follow straight through to take your opponent's elbow. When you have the elbow, you can step through and use the block as a throw if you want.

The upward block in action.

This block can also be used as a strike.

upper block

1 Start in the lower block position.

2 Step forward with your right leg and raise your right arm.

3 Cross your arms in front of your chest, with your right hand clenched into a fist.

4 Snap your right arm into position as you pull your left hand back to your belt.

kicking

If you look at the covers of most martial-arts books and magazines, you will see a picture of somebody executing a kick (geri). If you watch a martial-arts film, then the chances are that the hero will be a 'kicker'. (Indeed, some well-known martial-arts actors are renowned for their ability to perform high kicks on set.)

The simple reason for this is that kicks look good. A well-executed kick has an aesthetic quality that hints at the martial artist's power, balance and training.

But kicks don't just look good. In practical styles like karate, nothing is included for aesthetic reasons only. A good kick can be a fast and powerful attack that can cover a long range.

Look at the picture below. Here, one of the karateka is executing a forward punch. In terms of punching, this is the longest-range punch that there is. But look at the kick. A simple front kick hits the target and leaves the punching fist in mid-air.

Now think about the power behind the kick. Look at the muscles in your arms compared to those in your legs. Most people have at least twice the muscle development in their legs as in their arms. It comes in useful for walking!

But a kick is not just about the legs. You should use the whole of your body to drive power through a kick. You need to understand which part of the foot you are kicking with and the target area that you can hit with it.

The kicks that follow are some of the basic ones. Nearly all kicks can be performed as jumping kicks for added range and height. Some styles kick with the leading leg for extra speed, and others do not.

Karate teaches you which part of the foot it's best to kick with.

Kicks are an important aspect of karate. They help you to develop poise and suppleness. Kicking for a few minutes is also good cardiovascular training. Any karateka can vouch for that! However, do not be lured into thinking that karate is all about kicking. This is just one aspect of a varied art form.

front kick: mae geri

1	Contact area	the ball of the foot
2	Range	long
3	Power	high
4	Speed	fast
5	Difficulty level	easy
6	Suitability for sparring	highly suitable for free sparring

If you imagine a footballer taking a penalty, he will use a version of the front kick. The difference is that he will be kicking at the centre of a ball, that is, 15cm (6in) above the ground, and the karateka will be aiming at a much higher target.

The kick is fast, powerful and versatile. It can be aimed at either the middle section or the high section in sparring, and at the legs in self-defence.

Front-kick application.

The power of the kick comes from the hips, and not just from the flick of the knee. The knee is lifted quickly and the ball of the foot is shot outwards in a whiplash-type of motion. As you kick out with your foot, you simultaneously drive your hips forward for power. After the kick, it is important to bring your foot back as fast as you fired it out so that your leg cannot easily be caught and so that your knee is protected from damage.

When making the kick, you must use your hips to power your leg. If you can do this, then your kicks will develop great power.

Note that it is also possible to perform the front kick as a jumping kick.

1 Start in the fighting stance.

2 Step forward.

3 Lift your knee.

4 Kick out with the ball of your foot.

5 Withdraw your leg.

6 Now put your foot down in the fighting-stance position.

side-thrust kick: yoko geri kekomi

The side-thrust kick is a very powerful kick. In a way, it is like punching with the edge of your foot. The strength of your leg and the motion that is carried through from your body give the kick a powerfully piercing quality.

In traditional kata, the target for the side-thrust kick is frequently the neck. The neck is a target that would usually be avoided in sparring, however.

In sparring, side-thrust kicks can be used as straight kicks to the mid-section or head. The side-thrust kick is a useful technique for stopping an aggressive attacker. In sparring, some fighters consider attack the best form of defence. These fighters sometimes try to rush at their opponents, making it difficult for them to attack. One good way of stopping this sort of attack is with a well-placed side-thrust kick. Make sure that your balance is good, though, otherwise you may be knocked over!

The side-thrust kick can be performed in any stance. To execute it, the knee is raised and the kick is delivered by twisting the waist. As always, you should bring your foot back as quickly as possible after making the kick.

The side kick could also be used as a thrusting kick, depending upon the way that you use your kicking leg. For the thrusting kick, your body will usually lean into the kick more.

Side-thrust-kick application.

1	Contact area	the side of the foot
2	Range	long
3	Power	very high
4	Speed	fast
5	Difficulty level	medium
6	Suitability for sparring	highly suitable for free sparring

1 Start in the back stance.

2 Open your front foot.

3 Lift your knee in front of your body.

4 Pivot around on your standing leg.

5 Thrust your foot out with a twist of your hips.

6 Quickly bring your foot back again.

7 Put your foot on the floor.

8 Finish in the fighting stance.

kata

So far we have looked at a selection of the techniques that are used in karate. There are many more techniques, however, as well as different ways of performing a technique.

Who would have thought that there were so many variations of the punch? Indeed, skilled karateka can view most parts of their bodies as weapons. A little finger delivered to the correct place at the correct time, for example, can cause a devastating blow!

So how do we learn all of these techniques? One of the old ways was to learn just one technique and to practise it, sometimes for years, until the sensei or master was satisfied that the pupil was indeed ready to learn the next piece of karate knowledge.

Can you imagine trying to do that? Practising the same punch for about five years? These days, it simply would not happen. Techniques and methods have moved on. But think about the concept. There is a feeling within some karate schools, especially the more Zen-orientated ones, that this is not such a bad idea. If you have complete mastery of one technique, it will be devastating. And from that one technique, all of the other techniques will also flow.

As you can no doubt imagine, different masters had different ideas through the ages. Nowadays, most traditional martial arts use kata. Kata means 'pattern' or 'form'. Kata are used by nearly all of the other martial-art styles, no matter where they are from. Ju jitsu, judo, tai chi, wing chun and tae kwon do are just some that all regard kata as a basic building block, for instance.

Most of the kata have the 'one-technique' idea embedded in them. The old masters were very crafty when designing the kata. For example, our first kata, taikyoku shodan, is the key to mastering shotokan karate. If you can perform all of the techniques in this kata to a very high skill level, you will be an excellent karateka.

improving your kata

Engravings and murals show that kata were being practised around a thousand years ago. Many of the kata that exist today evolved from these old patterns and forms. And many of the techniques depicted are familiar to the modern martial artist.

Apart from learning something that stretches back into history, you are learning something that people have valued for an immensely long time in human terms. How much of today's culture will be similar in the year 3000?

For something to last that long, there must be some real substance to it, which surely makes it worth the effort of getting it right.

So what do we look for in our kata? In a very real way, the learning of kata is a spiritual experience. This is the dimension that transforms your kata into something worthwhile. In martial arts, the path to the spirit is the body. The different elements of the kata would have a lesser effect on their own. The joining of the elements leads to the transformation.

There are some things to focus on.

body alignment

Is your body aligned in the most efficient way? For example, if your front stance is leaning to one side, you cannot deliver maximum power. The laws of physics will be against you because gravity will always try to pull you into the worst direction for a karateka. If your body is in alignment, the energy meridians are open and ki can flow.

balance

The question of balance is related to body alignment. If your body is aligned, then it is balanced. But it is not just about your body. If your mind and body are not balanced, then you are not balanced physically. For example, if you are thinking about the next technique before finishing the one that you are performing, you will tend to lean into the technique, thus upsetting your alignment and balance.

If your technique is correct, and you are striking or blocking the correct parts, you are starting to control your body with your mind.

Smooth breathing and delivery of power are indications that you have started to balance such internal and external factors.

no mind

Balance leads directly to the concept of 'no mind', or 'the empty space'. In kata, you should think about the movement that you are performing. Not the one that you just did or the coming one. This means that you need to be balanced between the past and the future. This is what the meditation experts call the 'here and now'. Learning to experience the moment as it is leads to a profound state of meditation, and kata can help you to get there.

Do not mistake this for some kind of trance. The karateka must show very great spirit and an extreme level of alertness. The power of the kiai and the focus of the eyes are clear indicators that the spirit is strong.

first kata: taikyoku shodan

In the philosophy of karate, taikyoku represents the idea of the universe in its primal state. According to this concept, the universe started as a unity and split between heaven and Earth. Taikyoku represents that original state.

Taikyoku shodan therefore represents the karateka in the beginning stages. It is the most elementary of the katas, and therefore the most important. It is common for the karateka who reaches the black-belt level to revisit this kata. This gives more advanced students the chance to review their basic techniques in the light of a more complete understanding of the art.

The kata requires that you learn one block, one stance and one attack. The full kata, including transitional moves, is explained here.

1 Start in the ready stance.

2 Simultaneously look left, slide back your left foot, raise your left fist and project your right fist forward.

3 Twist your body into the front stance, while executing the left lower block.

4 Project your left fist and bring your right foot close to your left one. Clench your right fist near your belt.

5 Step into the front stance while punching with your right hand and pulling back your left fist for the right stepping punch.

6 Slide back your right foot as you look back over your right shoulder and raise your right fist. Project your left fist forward.

7 Turn through 180 degrees by twisting into a front stance while blocking downwards with your right hand for the right lower block.

8 Project your right fist forward as you bring your left foot close to your right foot. Keep your fists clenched.

9 Step forward with your left foot into the front stance. Use your left fist for a left stepping punch.

10 Step across with your left leg and turn to face forwards. Raise your left fist and extend the right.

11 Twist your body into the front stance and do a left lower block.

12 Step up with your right leg in preparation for punching.

13 Step forward in the front stance for the right stepping punch.

14 Step up with your left leg ready to punch with your left fist.

15 Step forward in the front stance for the left stepping punch.

16 Step up with your right leg to prepare for punching.

17 Move into the front stance for a right stepping punch. Shout 'kiai!'

18 Step across with your left leg in preparation for making a lower block to your left side with your left hand.

19 Execute a left lower block from the front stance.

20 Step up with your right leg ready to punch with your right fist.

21 Execute the right stepping punch in the front stance.

22 Slide back your right leg in preparation for an 180-degree turn and block.

23 Move into the front stance for a right lower block.

24 Step up with your left leg.

25 Step forward with your left leg and punch with your left hand for a left stepping punch.

26 Slide your left leg across in preparation for a lower block.

27 Twist into the front stance for a left lower block.

28 Step up with your right leg ready to punch.

29 Move your right leg into the front stance for a right stepping punch.

30 Step up with your left leg ready to punch.

31 Step into a left stepping punch in the front stance.

32 Step up with your right leg.

33 Perform a right stepping punch in the front stance with a loud 'kiai!'

34 Slide back your left foot in preparation for another lower block.

35 Execute a left lower block in the front stance.

36 Step forward to prepare to punch with your left fist.

37 Execute a right stepping punch with your right fist.

38 Slide back your right foot, turn through 180 degrees and prepare for a lower block.

39 Execute a right lower block in the front stance.

40 Step up with your left leg for a final punch.

41 Execute a left stepping punch.

42 Slide back your left foot level with your right.

43 Finish the kata in the finishing position.

kumite (sparring)

One of the useful things about the kata is that you can train on your own. You can work a little each day on the kata and then ask your sensei to correct any perceived imperfections.

This way of training on your own is very one-dimensional, however, and is certainly not what the spirit of karate is all about. To understand a technique, you need to practise it with somebody else. Practising your karate with a partner is called kumite, or sparring.

Kumite is performed on different levels. The first level is five-step sparring. In this, the karateka make five steps. Each step is an attack by one partner, with the receiving partner delivering a counterattack on the final attack. This approach teaches the karateka how to distance themselves and become accustomed to the idea of an attacker.

The next stage is three-step sparring. Three-step sparring follows the same pattern as five-step sparring, except that there are three steps instead of five. It is really a development of five-step sparring, and gives the karateka the chance to demonstrate more techniques in less time.

The final part of the choreographed sparring sequences is one-step sparring. In one-step sparring, one karateka attacks the other, who responds with a known technique. The emphasis here is on speed and accuracy.

Both karateka will know these choreographed sequences. There will be no contact, but the attacks and defences will be executed as though they were real. The fact that both karateka know what is going on gives them the chance to use maximum speed and power.

The final aspect of sparring is 'free sparring', or jiyu kumite. In jiyu kumite, the karateka try to attack each other in order to score points. Jiyu kumite gives the karateka the chance to test themselves. It is an excellent technique for sharpening skills, and the technique that is used for sport karate.

We will now examine some examples of the different sparring levels.

five-step sparring: gohon kumite

Apart from practising applications from the kata, gohon kumite is the first chance that a karateka has to practise his or her skill with another person. For this reason, the attacks are usually fairly straightforward.

That having been said, do not think that it can look sloppy. The spirit should be strong for both karateka. There should be a good 'kiai!' on the retaliation at the end of the sequence, and both karateka should maintain a high level of mental alertness and fighting spirit.

Do not make the mistake of walking through the practice with no real intent. Each punch should be performed as though it were real.

1 Start in yoi, the ready stance.

2 Bow.

3 Yoi (your partner should remain in yoi).

4 Step into the front stance; do a low block.

5 As your partner punches low, block with a low block. As your partner steps forward, step back. (Step one.)

6 As your partner punches low, block with a low block. As your partner steps forward, step back. (Step two.)

7 As your partner punches low, block with a low block. As your partner steps forward, step back. (Step three.)

8 As your partner punches low, block with a low block. As your partner steps forward, step back. (Step four.)

9 As your partner punches low, block with a high block. As your partner steps forward, step back. (Step five.)

10 Now retaliate with a reverse-section punch to the mid-section and shout 'kiai!'

other variations

Your karate club will have a syllabus of five-step sparring that you will have to learn for your grading. This can vary, depending on the style of karate that you are practising and who is teaching it. Some other common variations that you may want to try are these.

1 Steps with a low front kick and low block. Retaliate with a punch.

2 Steps with a middle punch and outer forearm block. Retaliate with a punch.

The list of variations could go on forever. Use your imagination!

three-step sparring: sambon kumite

The difference between sambon kumite and gohon kumite is that sambon kumite is performed on three different levels. This means that the attacks will be high, middle and low.

  The sequences are still prearranged. As with gohon kumite, clubs will have different sequences in their syllabuses. This example should be useful in giving you the gist of sambon kumite. It is always good to experiment, so try to make up your own sequences.

1 Start in yoi, the ready stance.

2 Bow.

3 Yoi (Steps 1 and 2 are only executed at the start of training with a new partner).

4 The attacker steps back in the front stance with a low block.

5 High punch with a high block.

6 Middle punch with an inner forearm block.

7 Front kick with a low block.

8 Retaliate with a reverse middle punch and a shout of 'kiai!'

free sparring: jiyu kumite

So far, all of the patterns and sparring techniques that we have looked at have been choreographed in one way or another. The purpose of so much choreographed work is to programme a set of responses into your body and mind. Then, if an attack comes, you do not need to think about what to do, you just do it.

Free sparring is an aspect of karate in which you test your responses. In free sparring, you have the opportunity to test your skills.

Free sparring is not a free-for-all. To avoid injury, we must follow very strict guidelines. Respect for your training partner is paramount. Under no circumstances should a fighter lose control. Karateka who become angry and try to hurt an opponent are showing how little they understand about their training!

Free sparring is popular because it can be used as a sport. This can lead karateka in a dangerous direction. By definition, sport has winners and losers: sport is all about competition.

To want to 'beat' your training partner in a sparring situation means that you want to be the 'best' in some way. This is an ego issue, and a common phrase in martial arts is, 'When you enter the dojo, leave your ego at the door'.

If you are sparring and your partner gets through your defences, this is actually a good thing. Think about it. How did it happen? Can he or she do it the next time? How do I stop him or her? Every time that your partner penetrates your defences, he or she has taught you something. Try not to let your ego get in the way and stop you from learning it!

free sparring

In a karate class, the most advanced form of free sparring is when two karateka are simulating a fight situation in a continuous practice fight. This is very different to real fighting in that there are rules. These rules are essential for the safety of the karateka. It is a mark of respect to both your fellow karateka and all that has gone before you in karate that you do not break the rules.

The rules of sparring vary from club to club, but essentially follow this concept.

Performed with respect for your fellow karateka, free sparring is an energetic and highly enjoyable way of learning karate. Just remember: you are there to learn, not to win.

Here are some images of free sparring.

1	No strikes below the belt.
2	No strikes to vital areas, such as the neck, kidneys or groin.
3	No strikes to the joints (elbows or knees).
4	No excessive contact.
5	No strikes to the head, unless headgear is worn.
6	Always wear groin protection and a gum shield.
7	Show respect for your partner. If you are more advanced than him or her, this is not an excuse for you to give your partner a bad time.
8	If the instructor shouts 'yame', you must immediately stop what you are doing. This rule is extremely important and overrides anything else that may be happening in the dojo.

Always bow first.

Adopt the fighting stance.

Turning kick.

Followed by a back kick.

Another turning kick performed with the other leg.

Retaliate with a high turning kick.

And another one.

Follow through with a lunge punch.

Attack with a spear-finger thrust.

Retaliate with a jumping front kick.

Fight back with another lunge punch.

Retaliate with a lunge punch.

Execute a hooking punch.

Retaliate with an elbow strike.

learning techniques for sparring

When you start to learn free sparring, you will usually be in a situation where there are more advanced karateka than you in the lesson. They are there to help you. They will remember what it feels like to be a beginner, and how ferocious a high-section side kick can look.

Use the situation. Remember that a more advanced student will not be perfect either. If you see an opening, take it, but keep your control. A frequent mistake for a beginner to make is to see an opening and not to show control. Remember that your sparring partners may have some tricks left up the sleeves of their gis!

As well as free sparring, the following two exercises are commonly used when practising sparring.

Firstly, only one person attacking and the other only blocking. This is a practice technique in which one karateka is on the attack and the other is only allowed to defend. The attacker knows that he or she is in no danger of being attacked, so can build up speed for the attack. This forces the defender to be very sharp when evading and defending.

Secondly, one-for-one free sparring. This is very similar to normal free sparring. As long as you stay within the rules of your dojo for sparring, you are encouraged to use any suitable technique. The difference is that you take it in turns to attack. This is an excellent way of building up your speed and stamina.

conclusion: so what *is* karate?

By this stage, you should have learned something about karate that has increased your understanding of karate's scope and definition. We have seen that it has many aspects that can all be expressed in different ways.

So what is karate? Is it a fitness system? A fighting system? A method for spiritual growth? A good way of defending yourself?

For a definition, let's look to someone who had a good idea, the founder of karate: Gichin Funakoshi. He once described karate as being like a mirror.

If you are preoccupied with violence, then you will see karate as a violent art form. If fitness is what you seek, you will see karate as a fitness session. If you are intent on spiritual growth, you will see karate as a vehicle for that growth.

Think about how you view the karate that you practise. Do you see yourself becoming fitter or more dangerous or working on your spirit? You cannot fool yourself because the only person who knows the real answer is you.

Just as we use a mirror in the bathroom to look at our exteriors, so we can use karate to view our interiors. If you can see what is going on inside yourself, you can work on changing it if you need to do so. In this way, karate can be an invaluable aid for learning more about yourself.

And in a way, that idea fits with the Zen roots of karate because karate just is!

judo

Judo means different things to different people; what it means to you depends very much on your reasons for taking part in judo and what you expect to gain from it. To some, judo is a fun activity, a competitive sport, a way of socialising or a fitness regime. To others, it is a means of self-defence, a way of challenging aggression or a form of combat. To experts, like Jigoro Kano himself, judo is a way of life.

Kodokan judo originated in Japan and owes its existence to Jigoro Kano, who was born in Mikage, Hyogo district, in western Japan on 28 October 1860. It has been said that Kano was physically weak in his early years and that he was the target of local bullies. This gave Kano an incentive to learn how to defend himself, and ultimately resulted in the development of judo.

At the age of 17, Kano moved to Tokyo, where he was introduced to Ryuji Katagiri, a ju jitsu teacher. However, Ryuji Katagiri believed Kano was too young for serious training and taught him only a few basic exercises. Not to be put off,

Kano found the dojo (school) of Hachinosuke Fukuda, who was a master in the Tenji-shinyo school of jujitsu. Master Fukuda had a different approach to Jigoro's former teacher, and encouraged him to practise randori (free-style fighting) rather than the kata (formal exercises) preferred by Katagiri.

A year after he began his ju jitsu training, Kano started attending the Tokyo Imperial University. In 1879, just one year after he had begun training at the Tenjin-shinyo school of ju jitsu, his master died. Kano's next instructor was Masatomo Iso, whose dojo was renowned for its excellence in kata.

Jigoro Kano absorbed himself in ju jitsu and practised whenever he could for the next two years. His sensei (coach) rewarded his dedication by making him an assistant and in 1881, at the age of 21, as well as graduating from Tokyo Imperial University, Kano became a master in Tenjin-shinyo-ryu ju jitsu. When his master, Masatomo Iso, became ill, Kano moved on in search of greater knowledge. He joined the Kito school of ju jitsu and trained under master Tsunetoshi Iikubo, who was highly skilled at teaching nage waza (throwing techniques) and opted for more free-style fighting.

the birth of judo

While Kano was at Tenjin-shinyo, his interest in developing a way to defend himself was stimulated still further. At the school he met Kenkichi Fukushima and, weighing about 55kg (100lb) less than Kenkichi Fukushima, Kano invariably lost any match against him. This frustrated Kano so much that he studied and trained even harder. He developed his own techniques and eventually defeated Kenkichi Fukushima with what he later called a kata guruma (shoulder wheel).

Initially, Kano had set about improving ju jitsu; it had not been his intention to develop a completely new system of self-defence. However, he had discovered weaknesses in ju jitsu and felt that he could develop his own ideas as a martial art, not only as a type of physical education, but also, more importantly, as a discipline of the mind and spirit.

The transition from ju jitsu to judo was by no means immediate. In February 1882, with nine of his private students from the Kito school, Kano started his own dojo in the Eishoji Buddist temple, based in the Tokyo district of Shitaya Inaricho. He named his new judo club the Kodokan. 'Ko' means to teach, study and learn, 'do' refers to the 'way' or 'path', and 'kan' means 'hall', so 'kodokan' literally means 'the place to learn the way of judo'.

Initially, in his Kodokan Kano Juku (academy), the training was mainly in ju jitsu. The Kito-ryu master, Iikubo, regularly visited and instructed Kano's students. It is not known exactly when the ju jitsu taught at Eishoji temple became judo, but it is possible that it coincided with the first time that Kano defeated his master, Iikubo, in randori.

a new way of thinking

To distinguish his new martial art and sport from ju jitsu, Kano called his system 'judo'. The literal translation of 'judo' means 'way of non-resistance', which is often simplified to 'gentle way'. In Kano's system, ukemi waza (break-fall techniques) were designed to add an element of safety, which in turn allowed greater progression in randori. Kano removed the elements of ju jitsu that he considered to be dangerous, eliminating most kicks, punches and strikes. Traditionally, most ju jitsu schools only practised kata (prearranged patterns of techniques) with co-operative partners. Now, Kano taught kata for skill acquisition, but also promoted randori, which offered a more realistic experience of unarmed combat.

However, the most significant difference between ju jitsu and judo lies with the do (way): to Kano, judo is a way of life. He developed what is known as kuzushi, the breaking of balance (which is what enabled him to defeat Master Iikubo). The principle is that a small amount of force is used to change an opponent's posture and draw them off balance, thereby allowing the opponent to be thrown. Kano maintained that this is possible regardless of whether the opponent is heavier. Put another way, Kano believed that one can maximise one's power by using one's brain. For example, when an opponent pushes, one should pull, and when an opponent pulls, one should push. As a result, control is gained over an opponent, irrespective of their size.

the growth of the school

Kano was a disciplinarian and tough on his students, but he was also a generous person: not wanting his poorer students to be at a disadvantage, he provided them with freshly laundered clothes to practise in.

In 1886, rivalry from local ju jitsu schools grew. This culminated in a grand tournament, overseen by the chief of Tokyo Metropolitan Police, between Kano's Kodokan and the Totsuka ju jitsu school. Kano could not afford for his team to lose, as defeat would diminish his credibility. However, he had nothing to worry about as his school won a decisive victory. Fifteen handpicked students from each school battled for supremacy. Kano's students won all but two contests, and those two were declared a draw. As a result, the Japanese government granted the Kodokan school official recognition.

The school changed addresses several times in the years that followed, as interest in the new sport grew and the need for larger premises arose. After just five years, the Kodokan school had over 1,500 members.

In 1889, hoping to make judo more popular throughout Japan, Kano turned his attention to sharing his knowledge with the rest of the world. The Kodokan school established the first gokyo (gokyo waza are the five sets, currently comprising forty throws, of kodokan judo) in 1895, which consisted of forty-two throws.

In 1909, the Kodokan became an official foundation, with a judo teachers' training department established in 1911. Kano travelled widely, telling people about his newly developed sport, and intended to create an international judo federation. The Dan Grade Holders' Association was developed in 1922, followed in 1932 by the Judo Medical Research Society. Prior to World War I, dojos were established in Britain, France, Canada, the United States, Russia, China and Korea.

Kano's lasting influence

Shortly after graduating from Tokyo Imperial University, Kano began teaching at Gakushuin school, and by the age of 25, he was appointed headmaster. Prior to Kano's appointment, Gakushuin was only attended by children from the imperial family and upper-class families. However, Kano refused to believe that academic potential was determined by status. He transformed Gakushuin into a boarding school, where he instilled discipline. Jigoro Kano's influence as headmaster of both Gakushuin and, in later years, the Tokyo Teacher-training School (now the Tokyo University of Education) shaped modern education in Japan.

In 1909, Jigoro Kano became the first-ever Japanese representative of the International Olympic Committee. Although there is no doubt that Kano's first love was judo, he was interested in all sports. He founded the Japan Athletic Association (JAA) in 1911, becoming the first president. He attended the 5th Olympiad in Stockholm in 1912, which was the first time that Japan had participated.

Although he was not totally against weight divisions in judo, Kano strongly believed that a small man is able to throw a large man with ease. Eventually, however, weight categories were introduced, initially with four weight categories at the Tokyo Olympics in 1964: lightweight, under 63kg (139lb);

middleweight, under 80kg (176lb); heavyweight, under 93kg (205lb); and the open weight.

Kano continued to teach and practise judo into the later years of his life – albeit with a more educational and spiritual focus as he no longer participated in randori himself.

Despite his efforts to promote Tokyo as a suitable host of the 1940 Olympic Games, World War II intervened and Japan had to wait until 1964 to become the host nation. Sadly, despite all of his efforts, Kano did not live to see his beloved judo become an Olympic sport. He died from pneumonia on 4 May 1938, aged 78.

However, his legacy continues: in 1952, Kano's dream of the International Judo Federation (IJF) became a reality; in 1956, Tokyo held the first world judo championships. Then, in 1964, when Japan hosted the Olympics, judo was included as an event for the first time, attracting 74 participants from 27 countries. There were just four weight categories and no women's competition. The Japanese dominated, but perhaps as a symbol of the growth of judo throughout the West, Anton Geesink, of The Netherlands, beat Akio Kaminaga, from Japan, in the final of the open weight-category.

women's judo (joshi judo)

It was not until 1923 that a women's section was formally established at the Kaiunzaka dojo. Formal tuition for women began in 1926, adopting a system that has become the basis of the present-day kodokan women's section. Initially, the women trained in kata and performed light randori; they were not permitted to engage in full-out randori as the men did.

Then, in 1980, the first-ever world judo championships open to women took place. Competitors entered from 27 countries. In the 1988 Seoul Olympic Games, women's judo was a demonstration event. Following its success, women's judo was eventually recognised by the International Olympic Committee and, in 1992, in Barcelona, the 25th Olympiad, women's judo at last became an event in its own right.

In shai, women compete against women and men compete against men. However, when they are training, men and women are often matched against each other.

fundamental aspects of kodokan judo

Judo is a Japanese martial art that is practised around the world by millions of people of all ages, races and physical abilities. It is equally suitable for men and women as it relies on technique rather than pure physical strength.

dojo and tatame

A dojo merely refers to the place where judo is practised. In this dojo is the tatame (mat). Throughout the years, the design of the tatame has advanced to enhance safety without inhibiting speed of movement.

Dojo training areas can vary dramatically in size, from 6 x 6m (20 x 20ft) to 100m² (390sq ft). A competition area is a minimum of 14 x 14m (46 x 46ft) and a maximum of 16 x 16m (53 x 53ft). This includes the red area (the danger area) and the safety area around the outside. Therefore, the actual contest area itself must be between 8 x 8m (26 x 26ft) and 10 x 10m (33 x 33ft).

judoka

A judoka is someone who participates in the martial art of judo. 'Uke' is the term used for the person being thrown. 'Tori' is the term for the person executing the technique.

judogi

Judogi represents clothing, that is the trousers, jacket and belt. Judo is practised wearing a judogi based on the theory that, if attacked, one's opponent is likely to be clothed. However, because everyday clothes would not be able to withstand frequent training sessions, a strengthened, double-weave jacket was designed.

etiquette

For reasons of hygiene, safety, self-discipline, respect and good sportsmanship, judokas are required to wear clean judogi, to ensure good personal hygiene, to have short nails, to tie back long hair and to have no footwear on the tatame, but to wear some form of zori (flip-flops) off the mat. There should be no unnecessary talking within the practice environment. Respect is a very important element in judo: a judoka should respect his or her sensei and other judokas. Rei is an expression of respect and consideration signified by a standing bow (ritsurei) or kneeling bow (zarei). A judoka performs a ritsurei when entering and leaving the dojo. A zarei is made as a group to the highest grade at the beginning and end of practice. A judoka always bows to an opponent before and after practice, and the same applies at a judo competition. The philosophy behind this is to show respect for your place of training, your sensei, your opponents and your sport.

ukemi waza (break-fall techniques)

Ukemi, or break-fall, techniques are moves that have been designed specifically to protect the body when being thrown. One of the major training aids for judo, these techniques are used by beginners and Olympians alike. They enable judokas to practise throwing each other on the tatame, and the action of the break fall avoids injury. The secret of any break-fall technique is being able to relax your body when being thrown. This comes with practice!

Usually, when practising break-fall techniques for the first time, they are performed close to the ground to lessen the impact and to allow the judoka to gain confidence and correct his or her technique before advancing to an upright position. It is important to learn break falls on both sides as you cannot choose which way an opponent will throw you. In order to learn these techniques correctly, beginners should seek the advice and guidance of a qualified judo sensei.

Note that the uke's hand is about to strike the mat, which absorbs the force of the throw, and that the tori supports the uke's landing.

side break falls

This is a single-arm break fall. A useful training drill for the side break fall can be done in pairs. The uke is on his or her hands and knees in a press-up position; the tori reaches under the uke's body, takes the far arm and pulls it through, maintaining the grip in order to support the uke. As the uke spins around, he or she slaps the mat in a side break fall.

NB: A major part of this training relies on the tori's support.

Stage 1
Note the body stance and hand preparation before the performance of the break fall.

stages 1 and 2

From a squatting position, the judoka pushes one leg across in front of the other and rolls on to his side.

stage 3

On making contact with the mat, the judoka slaps it with his free arm. Once confidence has been built, this can be performed from a standing position.

backward break fall

stage 1
The judoka lies flat on his back, knees bent and his back flat against the tatame. He places his arms across his body, and then slaps the mat, ensuring that he keeps his arms straight by his sides as he does so.

stage 2
The judoka then crouches down, with his arms straight by his sides (the tips of his fingers can be used to maintain his balance).

stage 3
He then rolls backwards, and, as his back touches the mat, slaps the mat with his hands.

forward-rolling break fall

Here, the action is similar to a forward roll, although, unlike in gymnastics, it is important that the head does not touch the mat for safety reasons. This type of roll is executed to the judoka's diagonal, and it is the shoulder, not the head, that makes contact with the tatame.

stage 1
Starting in an upright position, the judoka moves one foot forward (it is usually best to learn this on your dominant side first, and then to progress to the other side), and reaches forward with the arm on the same side.

stage 2
The judoka now turns his hand under, towards his own body. (It is advisable to take the advice of a judo sensei to ensure that this is done correctly.) The other hand can be used to assist balance.

stage 3
The judoka pushes off with the back leg, his shoulder makes contact with the mat and he slaps the mat.

grips and training

grips

A standard right-handed grip is where the tori holds the uke's right lapel midway above belt level with his or her right hand, thumb uppermost, while the left hand holds the sleeve below the uke's elbow. For a right-handed technique, the tori turns his or her body in an anti-clockwise direction.

For left-handers, or those who want to train on both sides, the left hand holds the lapel, again with the thumb uppermost, and the right hand holds the sleeve. A left-handed technique is generally done in a clockwise direction, although it is possible to hold right and throw left and vice versa. From the standard grip, a judoka can adopt a variety of grips, bearing in mind that penalties are given for non-standard grips, where a technique is not executed immediately. For example, if a judoka holds the

Left-handed grip.　　　　**Right-handed grip.**

trouser leg, belt or same side of the jacket with both hands and does not attack straightaway, a penalty will ensue.

traditional judo training methods

Judo starts with opponents taking hold of each other, so the distance between each judoka is usually arm's length. To be successful, a judo throw requires the space between judokas to be closed down, which is achieved by stepping towards each other, pulling and bypassing any blocks. The movement can be made in a one-step, two-step or three-step pattern, achieving body contact before lifting, and/or rotating and/or sweeping the opponent, causing him or her to lose balance.

It is important to practise the various aspects of traditional judo training. This is best achieved with a partner so that you can practise gripping, blocking and throwing each other in turn. To start with uchikomi, or skill-repetition work, involves positioning the body with various step patterns. Then kazushi is the technique of breaking an opponent's balance and nage komi is the completion of the throw.

one-step pattern
With a one-step pattern, the throwing position is achieved in one movement, which means that the throwing leg is also the stepping leg.

two-step pattern
This requires two steps to achieve the throwing position. The first step establishes positioning and the second step is also the throw.

three-step pattern
These are techniques that require three steps on entry into the technique. The first step is usually a step forwards. The second step repositions the body and the third step completes the throw.

competitive scoring

The objective of winning in the sport of judo is to throw an opponent with impetus onto his back.

ippon

Ippon actually means 'one whole point', but is given the value of ten points and an outright win. Ippon is signified by the referee raising his or her arm straight up in the air and simultaneously shouting 'ippon'. Ippon is achieved by throwing an opponent flat on his or her back with impetus; controlling him for 25 seconds in a recognised judo hold-down; obtaining a submission from a strangle or armlock; or if the referee sees fit to intervene. There is another way of achieving ippon: if a judoka gains two waza ari scores (see below), they combine to equal ippon.

waza ari

Waza ari is a seven-point score and is signified by the referee stretching out his arm at a 90-degree angle and calling 'waza ari'. Waza ari is given for something that is not quite an ippon. It is achieved when an opponent is thrown largely on to his or her back and/or without some of the impetus required for an ippon or by controlling an opponent on his back for 20 to 24 seconds.

yuko

A yuko is a five-point score. A referee signals a yuko by announcing 'yuko' and holding out a straight arm at a 45-degree angle from his leg. Yuko is achieved by throwing an opponent onto his side, but without speed and/or force, or by holding an opponent for between 15 and 19 seconds. Yukos are not accumulative, so regardless of the number of yukos scored, a waza ari is always worth more.

koka

A koka is a minor score, worth three points, shown by the referee bending his arm by his shoulder with an open hand and the palm facing forwards. A koka is achieved when an opponent lands on his or her buttocks, thigh or shoulder or when a osaekomi (a hold-down) is held for 10 to 14 seconds. As with yukos, kokas are not accumulative, so no amount of kokas are deemed equal to, or greater than, a yuko.

Scores are also awarded for shidos (penalties), which range from slight infringements to disqualifiable offences. If a competitor receives a shido, this becomes an equivalent positive score for his opponent.

If the time has elapsed and no outright win has been achieved, the winner of the contest is the competitor who has attained the highest of the above scores. However, if there are no scores, or the scores are drawn, the competitors move into the 'golden score'.

golden score

If, at the end of the allocated time, scores are equal, time is added (usually the duration of the contest) for a sudden-death round, where the first score wins, just like a golden goal in football.

If, within extra time, there is still no score, the two corner judges and the centre referee are required to make a decision by raising flags that correspond to the colour of the competitor's suit or belt, in support of the judoka whom they consider to be the closest to throwing or the one who made the most attacks. The winner is the one with the majority of flags in his or her favour.

officials

Generally, there is a centre referee and two corner judges, assisted by timekeepers and contest recorders, at each contest area. The time of a contest is usually 5 minutes for men and women and a shorter time, usually 3 minutes, depending on age, for juniors.

A gold medallist in a tournament would average six to seven contests within the day, depending on the fighting system used – a pool system or straight knockout.

grading and competition judo

The traditional way of progressing in judo is to train in three activities. The first is skill training and studying the intricacies of where and how to move the various parts of the body. The second is randori, free practice, where skills and techniques are tested out in relatively realistic situations. Thirdly, there is pro-active fighting in competition (shiai), where mistakes are costly to the outcome.

Not all judokas enter Olympic trials or major tournaments. Normally, their first experience of competition is at a judo grading. The judo grade system has been in existence since judo first began. Normally starting with a light, white-coloured belt, the belts grow darker as you progress through the grades and denote the skill, knowledge and experience of the wearer. The colours may vary slightly, but a normal system is: beginner belt white, then yellow, orange, green, blue and brown. These are called kyu, or beginner, grades. After brown comes the coveted black belt, the dan, or advanced grade.

A normal exam requirement would be for the judoka to fight opponents of the same or similar grades, and have knowledge of, and be able to demonstrate, specific judo techniques. This applies up to 5th dan black belt; obviously with the requirements becoming progressively more difficult. Above that grade, 6th dan changes to a red-and-white belt, eventually reaching 9th and 10th dan, when it becomes red. Normally, grades after 5th dan are awarded for time, knowledge, experience and service in the sport.

level	grade	
Beginner		white belt
5th kyu		yellow belt
4th kyu		orange belt
3rd kyu		green belt
2nd kyu		blue belt
1st kyu		brown belt
1st–5th dan		black belt
6th–8th dan		red-and-white belt
9th–10th dan		red belt

competition judo

If you are a competitor entering a judo event, you will fight in your weight category. Currently, in the Olympic games, there are seven different weight categories for men and women.

Contests are run using either a pool system, whereby competitors are put into groups and the top two from each group go through into the next round, or a straight knockout system, where competitors only progress to the next round if they win each fight. This includes a repecharge system, where competitors who lose to the semi-finalists battle it out for the bronze-medal positions.

Men:
under 60kg (132lb); under 66kg (145lb); under 73kg (160lb); under 81kg (178kg); under 95kg (209lb); under 100kg (220lb); over 100kg (50lb)

Women:
under 48kg (105lb); under 52kg (114lb); under 57kg (125lb); under 63kg (138lb) under 70kg (154lb); under 78kg (39lb); over 78kg (39lb)

kata

Traditionally handed down through the centuries, kata training is a style of judo training that involves specific movements with no variation. They contain idealised, set patterns of techniques that depict specific judo principles.

The set patterns are not demonstrated in this book, as it focuses on a more competitive style of judo.

There are seven formal katas in judo, for which see the chart on the right.

randori

Randori is free practice or free sparring without the presence of referees, allowing the judoka to practise in a relatively realistic (to competition) situation. All of the techniques in this book can be used in randori and competition.

Nage no kata: a set of kodokan judo formal throwing techniques.

Katame no kata: a set of kodokan judo formal groundwork techniques.

Go no sen no kata: a set of kodokan judo formal counter-throwing (reactive) techniques.

Koshiki no kata: a set of kodokan judo formal techniques. These are the classic forms that were inherited from the Kito-ryu ju jitsu school.

Kime no kata: a set of kodokan judo formal techniques designed to teach the fundamentals of defence against an attack. These attacks are throwing, grappling and striking techniques. Sometimes known as the self-defence form.

Itsutsu no kata: a set of five kodokan judo formal techniques used to express principles of attack and defence.

Ju no kata: a set of kodokan judo formal techniques formulated to allow judokas to practise judo moves without a judogi or a judo dojo. They are forms of flexibility and gentleness.

nage waza (throwing techniques)

'Nage waza' is the Japanese term for throwing techniques. To avoid confusion, all throws in this book are demonstrated to the right. If you are left-handed, simply reverse the hand positions and direction of the turn (if applicable) shown. In fact, it is useful to practise the techniques on both sides as this helps to prevent any muscular imbalance and also serves to confuse one's opponent. For easy understanding of the techniques in this book, the tori is always wearing blue and the uke wears white.

kazushi

It is important to realise that judo is not all about brute strength. An important lesson in judo is that of kazushi, the action of breaking an opponent's balance in preparation for the throw. Initially, a judoka develops a feel for an opponent's weaknesses. This is done by the tori moving around the mat, pushing and pulling the uke until there is a state of imbalance. The tori must capitalise on this imbalance and know when to attack and in which direction. This is best achieved by using an opponent's resistance to a push or a pull and throwing in the direction of that resistance.

The techniques in this section are listed in alphabetical order. To assist you in using the book and in locating certain types of technique, however, the throws have been categorised on the following pages into foot or leg techniques, hip techniques, hand techniques and sacrifice techniques.

ashi waza (foot or leg techniques)

kosoto gari (minor outer reap)

Grip: The most effective grip for this technique is a middle to high lapel and low sleeve grip.

Entry and execution: Usually a one-step entry is used. The sole of the tori's right foot connects with the uke's heel, to the outside of the uke's left leg, and sweeps in the direction of the uke's toes. The hands control the uke and prevent her trying to turn out, ensuring that the uke's body weight is pulled over the removed leg, causing her to lose balance and fall back to the mat.

Opportunity for attack: Opportunity for this technique arises if the uke is slightly sideways on and steps forward with her left foot. The tori can also create his own opportunity by adjusting himself to carry out the technique.

Related techniques: Kosoto gake.

Possible combinations and counter techniques: Kosoto gari into tani otoshi; kosoto gari countered by uchimata.

1 This shows the grip and the uke's forward foot placement.

2 This demonstrates the foot placement and hand control.

3 This shows the sweeping action and hand control required to complete this technique.

osoto gari (major outer reap)

Grip: The most effective grip for this technique is a high lapel and low sleeve grip, although a mid-lapel and low sleeve grip can also be effective.

Entry and execution: Initially, the tori steps forward with her left leg towards the uke's right foot, placing her left foot level, or just past, the uke's right foot. (The tori allows enough space for her right leg to go through between the outside of the uke's right leg and the tori's own left leg.) The tori's hips should be slightly rotated and hooking the back of the uke's thigh. The sweeping action is executed following the breaking of balance to the uke's rear right corner. The tori's head and the heel of her sweeping leg should be parallel, therefore the lower the head, the higher the heel should go. To complete the technique, the tori's right leg connects with the back of the uke's right leg and the tori lowers her head and drives back and down with her hands.

Opportunity for attack: Osoto gari is most successful against an opponent with an upright posture and when the uke's feet are level or the attacked leg is a bit back.

Related techniques: Osoto gake.

Possible combinations and counter techniques: Osoto gari to nidan kosoto gari; osoto gari to yoko wakare.

1 This shows the high lapel and low sleeve grip.

2 This shows the first step and the breaking of balance to the uke's rear.

3 This demonstrates the position of the throwing leg.

4 This shows the completion of the technique by lifting the throwing leg.

koshi waza (hip techniques)

hane goshi (hip spring)

Grip: A high lapel or over the shoulder and low sleeve grip. The main objective of this high grip is to aim for chest contact.

Entry and execution: The tori uses a two-step entry, stepping in with the right leg and swinging the left leg behind to become the support leg. The tori does not quite make a full turn with his body, so allowing enough space to lift the right leg and prop it, in a bent position, against the uke's right leg, so that it acts as a platform. The tori pulls the uke's sleeve round in a semi-circular action and rotates the upper body. The spring element refers to the straightening of the support leg and the pushing of the bent, platform leg.

Hane goshi is sometimes mistaken for uchimata. However, if done correctly, the tori uses the leg as a prop and pushes the uke's leg in a sideways direction rather than swinging the leg backwards, as in uchimata.

Opportunity for attack: This throw can be used when the uke is in a slightly bent posture, with the uke standing still or moving backwards, used as a catch-up movement.

Related techniques: Hane makikomi.

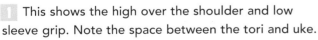

1 This shows the high over the shoulder and low sleeve grip. Note the space between the tori and uke.

2 This demonstrates the positioning of the leg and the close body contact.

3 This demonstrates the lifting action of tori's leg.

4 This shows the rotation of the shoulders required.

sode tsurikomi goshi (sleeve lift-pull hip throw)

1 sleeve and lapel grip

1 The single sleeve and middle lapel grip.

2 The tori is pushing the sleeve up and stepping across the front of the uke at the same time.

3 This demonstrates the body positioning.

4 This shows the rotation required in order to complete both throws.

Grip: The tori can use a middle lapel and low sleeve grip or a double sleeve grip.

Entry and execution: The best entry is a one-step. The tori takes a sleeve and lapel grip. If he wanted to turn right, the tori would take a left-handed grip because, with this technique, he pushes the sleeve arm across the uke's body and anchors on the lapel. The uke is forced over the tori's hips. Alternatively, the tori can work from both sleeves, pushing the uke's sleeve up above his shoulder line, breaking the uke's grip, then rotating his hips across. The tori pulls one sleeve down and the other up, and the uke is rotated over the tori's hips.

Opportunity for attack: This throw works well against a uke with a high lapel and sleeve grip with an upright posture (the uke's grip is broken as the arm is pushed across the body).

2 double sleeve grip

1 The double sleeve grip.

2 The tori pushes the uke's sleeve up and simultaneously steps across.

3 This shows the tori's body positioning.

te waza (hand techniques)

ashi dori (leg grab)

Grip: The tori can use either a sleeve and lapel grip, removing the sleeve grip on entry, or just take the one lapel.

Entry and execution: The tori uses the lapel grip and comes directly in for the attack, or uses a sleeve and lapel grip and lets go of the sleeve grip on entry. The uke has his weight on the back leg and so is caught off guard. The tori bends her knees to lower her stance, still maintaining the lapel grip, reaches for the uke's far leg and either grips the trousers or cups the leg and drives her weight forward, taking the uke to the ground, pushing back and down with the lapel grip. There is a variety of leg grabs: for example, the tori can grip the lapel and leg on the same side of the uke, or on opposite sides, on the inside or outside of the leg.

Opportunity for attack: This technique is usually used when the uke has his weight on the back leg.

Related techniques: Morote gari or te otoshi.

1 The single-hand lapel grip leaves the other hand free to execute the technique.

2 This demonstrates the hand placement on the outside of the knee.

3 This demonstrates the hand control required to ensure that the uke lands on his back.

ippon seoi nage (one-arm shoulder throw)

Grip: There are several ways of gripping for ippon seoi nage. The tori can start with a double middle lapel grip or a middle lapel, low sleeve grip, but ultimately the tori's right arm is placed under the uke's right armpit. The tori's other hand can be attached to the uke's sleeve or lapel.

Entry and execution: Ippon seoi nage is a very versatile throw, combining well with many other techniques. The tori takes a two-step entry, stepping forward with his right foot and swinging the left foot behind. His feet are about a shoulder-width apart.

1 This shows the low sleeve grip on the arm to be attacked.

2 This demonstrates the arm placement and body position required.

3 This shows the rotation of the tori's shoulders to complete the technique.

The tori's back remains straight as his knees are bent, bringing his waist below the uke's. The uke's belt level is a good guideline, the aim being for the tori's belt level to be lower than the uke's. The tori places his right arm under the uke's right armpit, with the inner elbow joint in the uke's armpit region; this arm is used as a prop. The tori pulls the uke on to his back, using either a sleeve or lapel grip, then straightens his legs and rotates his upper body, pulling in a big circular movement to offload the uke.

Opportunity for attack: This works better on an uke with a slightly bent posture. It can be adapted to work off both knees.

Related technique: Morote seoi nage.

Possible combination techniques: Ippon seoi nage into kata guruma; ippon seoi nage into kouchi gake; ippon seoi nage into seoi otoshi; and ippon seoi nage into uchi makikomi.

sutemi waza (sacrifice techniques)

hane makikomi (springing wraparound throw)

Grip: Initially, a high lapel and low sleeve grip is established. However, to complete this technique, the lapel grip is removed and wound around in a circular motion above the uke's right arm.

Entry and execution: The tori steps in using a standard right-handed grip. As with hane goshi, the right foot is followed by the left, which becomes the supporting leg and the right leg is used as a prop. The lapel grip is then removed. It is the change of grip that transforms what would be hane goshi into hane makikomi; greater body contact is achieved and a winding action is adopted to complete the throw. The technique is completed with a lifting action from the propping leg and a winding action of the body to the ground.

Opportunity for attack: This technique works well when the uke is preventing the tori from gaining a right-handed lapel grip and/or is controlling the left sleeve.

Related techniques: Harai makikomi; osoto makikomi; soto makikomi; uchimata makikomi; and hane goshi.

1 This shows the low sleeve and the first attack position of the free arm.

2 This shows the leg and body position required with the start of the action.

3 This shows the lifting action of the legs and the rotation required to complete the technique.

tomoe nage (circular throw)

Grip: This is executed using a mid-lapel and low sleeve grip.

Entry and execution: Tomoe nage is often referred to as 'the stomach throw'. This technique is a rather spectacular throw when executed correctly, and it is for this reason that it is often featured in fight scenes in action movies. Tomoe nage is, however, a sacrifice technique, and therefore should be attempted with extreme caution: a failed tomoe nage could result in one's opponent gaining the score (usually ippon, as the tori puts herself straight on to her own back). The tori uses a one-step entry, initially placing her left foot between the uke's legs and pulling forwards with the arms to break the uke's balance. Her right foot is placed on the uke's stomach at belt level, and the tori drops to the mat, aiming to get her backside as close to the uke as possible. The tori pulls the uke forward, on to her foot, and rolls backwards, taking the uke over her head.

Opportunity for attack: This technique is ideal against a uke with a bent posture or if the tori's head is being pulled down.

Related techniques: Sumi gaeshi.

1 The uke has a jigota (bent-over) posture.

2 The tori drops underneath the uke, pulling down the upper body and placing her foot on the uke's stomach.

3 The tori uses her hands and foot to direct the uke on to his back to complete the throw.

tachi waza
(combination and counter techniques)

If a judoka were to use the same technique all the time, he or she would become predictable and easy to defeat through a counter-manoeuvre. There is a need, therefore, for a judoka constantly to add to his or her repertoire by combining one technique with another or more.

All of the techniques shown in this book can be used in combination and are referred to by the group names renzoku waza (see pages 72–73) and renraku waza (see pages 74–75). The objective is to employ the principle that any action creates a reaction. Therefore, if the tori attacks the uke, the uke will either defend or block against it, will move away from it, or will have to change his or her stance in expectation of an attack. Different techniques are then combined to capitalise on the way that the uke moves.

The combinations demonstrated here are generally one technique into another. However, a judoka may link two, three or four techniques together in an attempt to outwit an opponent. Equally, combinations do not necessarily follow on from each other, but become a successive run of one judoka countering the action of the other and so on. A good judoka will be able to accomplish instantaneous, explosive techniques, but will also use combination and counter techniques to add an element of successful unpredictability.

There are three tactics involved in using combination techniques, as outlined below.

body-contact waza

The tori attacks to achieve body contact and maintains it as the uke resists and reacts. The tori moves to the second waza as the uke's resistance has placed his body in a more unstable position.

a feint

This requires the tori to make an action that sets his opponent up for a certain throw, while moving into another. The feint must be convincing, otherwise the essential element of surprise will be lost. Another way that a feint can be used to provoke a reaction is for the tori just to pull or push forwards, backwards or to the side. The uke's reaction is normally to resist in the opposite direction to which he is being pushed or pulled, often then coming off balance. The tori then switches to a second technique, usually in the direction of the uke's movement.

time-phase combination

This tactic requires a strong attack, or multiple attacks, of a particular waza. If the uke's reaction is to change his posture or grip to nullify expectations of the same, or similar, attack, the tori can launch a sudden attack of a totally different waza. By doing this, he is able to take advantage of the now weaker posture that the uke has developed in defending against the same waza for a long time.

renzoku waza

Renzoku waza are standing techniques used in combination, where the second technique is a continuation of the first carried out in the same, or a similar, direction. Renzoku waza work on the basis that the tori is really committed with the initial attack, but has been unsuccessful as a result of the uke's defence. Because the tori has concentrated all of his efforts in that direction, the second technique has to be in the same direction. Alternatively, the tori may deliberately set out to fool his opponent with the initial technique, with the intention of moving into the second move when the uke is caught off guard. Examples of renzoku waza are as follows.

harai goshi into soto makikomi
(hip sweep into outside winding)

The tori adopts a low sleeve and high lapel grip. He steps across, blocking the back of the uke's thigh with his thigh, and pulls the uke forward. The uke's reaction is to block with the hips. The tori then pushes his hips further through, lets go of the uke's neck, and wraps his arm over the arm that he is already holding. The tori then rotates into the ground to complete the soto makikomi counter.

1 This shows the high collar and low sleeve grip.

2 This shows the tori's body placement and the uke's blocking action.

3 The tori's grip changes to a winding arm.

4 This shows the falling action and the required rotation of the body and arm in order to complete the technique.

ippon seoi nage into kata guruma
(one-arm shoulder throw into shoulder wheel)

This is a body-contact technique. The tori turns in for a one-arm shoulder throw, using a two- or three-step entry. He pushes his hips too far through, so his shoulders are in contact with the uke's body. He then reaches through and hooks the uke's leg with his other hand, pulling the uke on to the top of his shoulder. He lifts the uke off the mat and rotates him onto his back.

1 This shows the single-hand grip over the uke's arm on to the lapel.

2 This shows the position required for the ippon seoi nage *waza*.

3 This shows the change of back placement for the kata guruma.

4 This shows the lifting action and hand placement.

5 This shows the direction of the throw that completes this technique.

renraku waza
(throws in the opposite direction)

Renraku waza are combinations of throwing techniques executed in rapid succession without a break, where the second technique takes advantage of the reaction of an opponent and throws him in a completely different direction. These are throws in opposite directions, using the principle that any action by the tori will get a reaction from the uke. Examples of renraku waza that work in competition follow.

deashi barai into tomoe nage
(advancing foot sweep into circular throw)

1 This shows the middle lapel and low sleeve grip.

2 The tori's deashi barai attack.

3 The uke's reaction is to step back.

4 The tori's follow-up: the tomoe nage foot position.

This is normally a one-step action. The tori touches the advanced foot with the sole of his front foot, which, to be effective, the uke must believe to be a side-sweep attack. The uke steps back and, simultaneously, the tori pulls forward and places the sweeping leg on the uke's stomach. The tori drops on to his back, taking the uke over in a full circle.

5 This shows the throwing position of the tori's body.

6 This demonstrates the circular action of tomoe nage at the completion of the throw.

ippon seoi nage into kouchi gake
(one-arm shoulder throw into minor inner hook)

1 Grip.

2 Feint.

3 Body position.

The aim of the initial technique is to achieve body contact, using the one-arm shoulder throw technique, which requires the tori to grip either the sleeve or the lapel. (This tends to be more successful with the lower sleeve grip, although the lapel has a higher surprise element.) The tori initially takes a two-step entry inside the uke's leg using a lunging action, but rotates his head and shoulders towards the uke's front. The tori's back is in contact with the uke's chest, and the inner part of his elbow joint is under the uke's armpit. This convinces the uke that ippon seoi nage is about to take place. The tori's inside leg hooks on to the uke's leg and the tori drives back off his back leg, the supporting leg. This action is done as the uke defends and pushes his hips forward and leans backwards, making himself more susceptible to the rear attack.

4 Throw.

kaeshi waza

These are countering techniques. If you are attacked, you must take action, whether it be to block the technique, move out of the way or, preferably, to convert it to your advantage. If you do nothing, you will be thrown! A judoka should practise counter throws so that they become second nature. As soon as an opponent comes in for a technique, it should be anticipated and countered. However, if a competitor merely waits for an opponent to attack so that he or she can counter, he or she runs the risk of receiving a penalty for passivity. Kaeshi waza are counter techniques within judo. For every technique with which you are attacked, there is a possible counter.

A counter is a tactic where the uke positions his body and gripping pattern, setting a trap for the tori, hoping that the tori will attack so that the uke can win with a counter, becoming the tori. To save confusion, although an attacking judoka is normally referred to as 'the tori', and the judoka being thrown is 'the uke', in this section of the book, 'the tori' indicates the judoka who makes the counter and throws. 'The uke' refers to the judoka being countered, despite his original attack.

ashi guruma countered by te guruma (leg wheel countered by hand wheel)

The uke attacks with ashi guruma, his front leg coming across the tori's thighs. The tori lets go of his sleeve grip, lowering to take the inside of the tori's attacking leg's thigh. The tori maintains the lapel grip. He then bends his knees, simultaneously pulling the uke on to him, and lifts. At the peak of the lift, the tori pulls the lapel towards him. This rotates the uke into a position flat on his back. This is also a useful counter against a harai goshi attack.

1 The tori takes a mid-lapel and low sleeve grip.

2 This shows the uke's ashi guruma attack.

3 This shows the tori's block and hand placement.

4 This shows the tori's lifting action.

5 This shows the direction required for the completion of the te guruma.

osoto gari countered by osoto gaeshi
(major outer reap counter)

The tori positions her front leg close to the uke's front leg, setting a trap for the uke's closest leg to attack the tori's front leg by placing his leg behind the tori's. It is vital that the uke has no control over the tori's head. The tori's free leg swings around in a rear half-circle and becomes weight-bearing. The attacked leg becomes the sweeping leg and completes the technique.

1 This shows the high collar and low sleeve grip.

2 The uke's osoto gari attack.

3 The tori breaks the uke's balance with leg placement.

4 This shows the lifting leg action required.

5 This demonstrates the full action of osoto gaeshi at the completion of the technique.

newaza (ground techniques)

The object of judo is to score ippon (see page 60). This can be achieved by throwing one's opponent flat on his back with impetus. However, it can also be achieved on the ground, by gaining a submission or by holding one's opponent on his back for 25 seconds (using an accepted method).

If an opponent is immobilised for 25 seconds, ippon is awarded, and this immediately finishes the contest. Lesser scores are achieved for shorter periods of holding. For example, after 10 seconds, a koka is scored, after 15 seconds, a yuko is scored, and after 20 seconds, a waza ari is scored.

A submission also finishes the contest immediately. This can be accomplished by an armlock, which may only be applied to the elbow joint, or by a strangle or choke on the neck. The uke signifies submission to a technique by tapping either the tori or the tatame twice with his hand. The foot can be stamped in submission if the uke's arms are trapped, and, as a last resort, the uke can call 'matte' ('submit'). It should be stressed that the objective is to gain submission, not to harm one's opponent. Judo students are trained to submit before damage can occur.

The Japanese word 'gatame' is found in the names of both hold-downs, such as hon kesa gatame, and armlocks, such as ashi gatame. It actually means 'to tighten', and, interestingly enough, originally holds were not timed; instead, the aim was to gain a submission.

In newaza (ground techniques), the uke will often adopt a defensive posture. This could be flat on his front or on his hands, or, more likely, elbows, and knees (this is often referred to as the 'all-fours' position). Much groundwork capitalises on the uke's defensive posture. Turn-overs have been developed from these positions to obtain holds, armlocks and strangles. Some armlocks and strangles can be applied directly from these positions. Another common position is for the uke to have one or both legs trapped between the tori's. The uke is usually kneeling, otherwise 'matte' is called and both parties stand up.

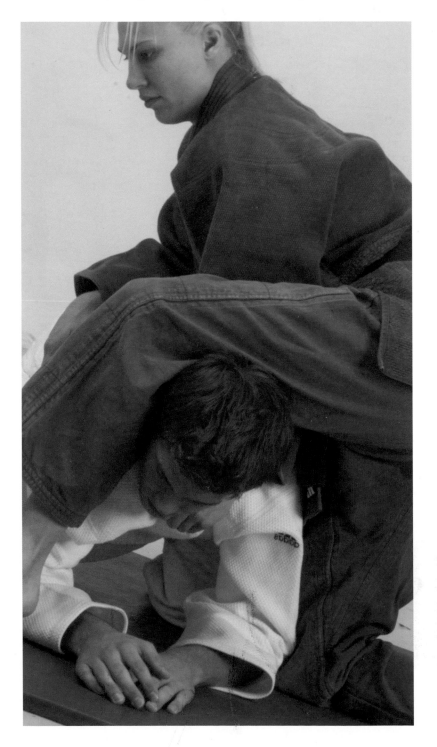

osaekomi waza (hold-downs)

Please be advised that the holds that follow are demonstrated, in most cases, purely as holds using a co-operative uke lying on his back. Anyone who has partaken in randori or contest judo will know that it is simply not that easy to get one's opponent into this position. There are infinite ways to get an opponent into a hold-down, and, where possible, suggestions have been made.

hon kesa gatame (basic scarf hold)

Hon kesa gatame is quite a versatile hold-down. It can be used from a variety of throws, especially those using a high lapel grip. This is because very little adjustment is required and the uke lands in a holding position. There are many newaza turn-overs that result in hon kesa gatame, which is what makes it such a popular and effective technique.

When learning hon kesa gatame, the tori begins by sitting next to the uke almost with her back to the uke, but slightly turned towards the uke's head. The arm nearest the uke's head (for a right-handed technique this will be the right arm) is placed around the uke's neck (like a scarf) and grips the jacket around the lapel or shoulder region.

The uke's right arm is placed under the tori's left armpit and squeezed tightly to maintain control. The tori leans on the uke's upper body. The tori's legs are spread in a hurdle-type position, ensuring that her back leg is not trapped by the uke, breaking the hold-down. The tori's legs stabilise the uke and help to prevent the tori being turned off the uke.

kami shiho gatame (upper four-quarters hold)

This hold, as its name suggests, controls the uke's upper body. Kneeling just above the uke's head, the tori slides his arms under both of the uke's shoulders and grips the belt. The tori achieves chest contact at the same time. If the tori pulls the belt towards himself, the hold is tightened. The uke's head is under the tori's armpit. The tori pushes his

stomach and hips to the floor and spreads his legs out straight, feet wide apart, using his toes to push off the mat and assist his control of the uke. This technique can also be applied with the knees bent up, close to the uke. In a contest situation, the tori may find it necessary to vary the leg position to counter the uke's struggle to escape.

kata gatame (shoulder hold)

This is normally used as a continuation from hon kesa gatame (see page 79), although it is a technique in its own right. If, from a hon kesa gatame position, the uke manages to release his right arm, he will push the tori's chest or neck in an attempt to escape. The tori utilises the uke's struggle by pushing the uke's arm across his own face and placing her own neck or the side of her face against the tricep area of the uke's arm. She then takes hold of the hand that is around the uke's neck and applies pressure. The legs can be in a hurdle position on the mat, as in hon

kesa gatame, or can be strengthened by coming on to the nearest knee with the other leg out straight and the foot pushing against the tatame for stability.

To prevent the uke from escaping, a helpful tip would be for the tori to release the grip with her left hand and pass her own lapel to the right hand. This secures the hold, but also allows the tori to use her free (right) hand to maintain her balance as the uke struggles.

shime waza (strangles/chokes)

The principle of a strangle or choke is to apply pressure to the carotid artery located at either side of the neck – this cuts off, or slows down, the blood supply to the brain – or to put pressure on the windpipe, which shuts off the air supply to the lungs. In a contest, or randori, situation, an initial strangle to the carotid artery may turn into a choking action on the windpipe or vice versa. Irrespective of the application, both achieve the same result in sport judo terms: they gain a submission (or referee's intervention) and an outright win. Referees are aware of the dangers of such a situation, and can call ippon if they believe that the uke is in danger of becoming unconscious.

Accuracy of the hand placement when executing a stranglehold is vital to the success of the technique. The legs very often assist in controlling an opponent. Safety is an important issue, as these techniques can cause dizziness, unconsciousness and, potentially, death. All judoka are trained to signal submission before any damage occurs.

Within this section, reference will be made to the 'cutting edge' of the arm; this merely refers to the inner, bony part of the forearm, which digs into the neck when applying a stranglehold.

gyaku juji jime (reverse cross strangle)

Gyaku juji jime requires the tori to have the fingers of both hands inside the lapels of the uke's jacket. His arms should be crossed at the wrists, with the back of one wrist against the front of the other. His fingers should be pushed deep enough into the jacket to enable the cutting edge of the wrist to touch the carotid-artery area. If the tori pulls down and then pushes out, he pushes the muscles that protect the carotid artery to one side, and this should result in immediate submission (1–4 seconds). If an immediate submission does not occur (up to 10 seconds), this means that the wrist action is not accurately on the carotid artery. This strangle is usually applied when the tori is on his back and the uke is between his legs, or if the tori is sitting astride the uke in a tate shiho gatame position.

Gyaku juji jime, kata juji jime and nami juji jime are all very similar strangles and differ only in the way that the lapel is gripped.

hadaka jime (naked strangle)

This is a neck choke. The reason that it is 'naked' is because no element of the judogi is used. This means that there are many varieties of strangles that don't use the cloth of the judogi, which are all called hadaka jime. Two of them are described below.

version 1

This requires the tori to be behind the uke, sliding his arm around to the front of the uke's throat. The inside of the elbow should be level with the front-middle section of the uke's neck, and the arm should be bent. The cutting edge of the tori's forearm is level with one side of the carotid artery, while the bicep muscle targets the other. To apply pressure, the tori grasps the bicep of his own opposite arm and places that arm behind the back of the uke's head, pushing forward with his chest and squeezing his arms together.

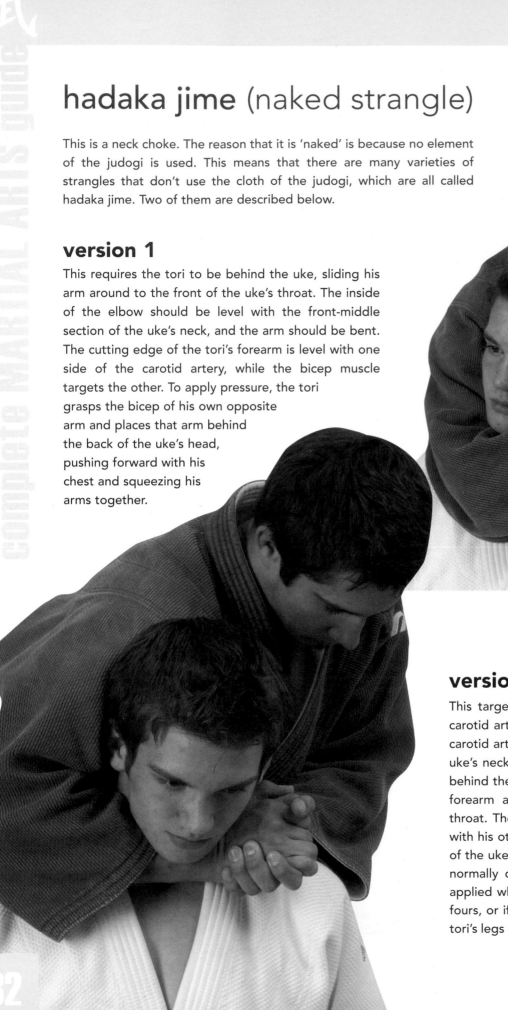

version 2

This targets the windpipe area initially, rather than the carotid artery, although it can also apply pressure to the carotid artery, depending on the size and strength of the uke's neck and/or the amount of pressure applied. From behind the uke, the tori positions the cutting edge of his forearm against the front-middle section of the uke's throat. The tori then holds the hand of the strangle arm with his other hand and places his chest against the back of the uke's neck or shoulder. As with all strangles, this is normally done in ground grappling (newaza). It can be applied when the uke is defending on his front, or on all fours, or if the uke is rolled over, ending up between the tori's legs (with both judokas facing in the same direction).

kansetsu waza (armlocks)

In judo, as with a strangle, an armlock is normally used in ground techniques (newaza). The objective is to apply pressure on the elbow joint. In sport judo, armlocks to joints other than the elbow joint are forbidden. It is also prohibited to throw someone being held with an armlock because the element of control is removed and the uke is highly susceptible to injury.

It is often difficult to tell where the elbow joint is under an opponent's judogi. A helpful tip when applying an armlock that involves straightening the arm is to pull in the direction of the little finger. That is, if the little finger is down (and the thumb up), take the arm down. Also bear in mind that you may have to make slight adjustments to counteract the independent wrist movement.

ashi gatame (leg armlock)

This technique is applied when the uke is between the tori's legs. If the uke takes a lapel grip on the tori's jacket, the tori manoeuvres onto his own hip, simultaneously pulling the uke's arm and following his leg over the arm, placing the foot under the uke's chin.

hara gatame (stomach armlock)

This technique is attempted when the uke is in a defensive posture, on her hands and knees. The tori hooks his heel onto the inside of her elbow, drawing the arm out with the heel to straighten it. At the same time, he pushes his stomach into the uke's shoulder. Invariably, the uke will collapse onto her front. The tori then crosses the hooking leg over to his other leg, maintaining pressure on the uke's shoulder with his stomach.

hiza gatame (knee armlock)

This armlock is applied when the uke is between the tori's legs and is using a lapel grip to push her hands into his chest. The tori grabs the uke's wrist and manoeuvres on to his furthest hip, simultaneously pulling the arm straight. This can be very fast and effective if, as the tori turns onto his side, he uses his foot to push the uke's knee back, causing her to collapse. The tori then places his knee on her elbow area, exerting pressure with his leg and arm to apply the armlock.

juji gatame (cross armlock)

This is usually applied with the uke on her back, but can be done in an upside-down position. There are many entries for juji gatame, ranging from turn-overs to the extravagant transfer from tomoe nage into juji gatame. The cross element refers to the tori's legs, which are placed across the uke's body. This positioning gives the tori a good degree of control over the uke. With the uke on her back, the tori anchors onto her arm. With his legs on either side of the uke's arm, the tori holds the arm secure with his thighs. Applying pressure to the joint, the tori uses his body weight to control a resisting uke. He extends the arm, holding both hands on her wrist, and uses the groin area as a fulcrum. This applies pressure on the uke's elbow joint. If necessary, the tori raises his hips to increase the leverage on the arm.

newaza
(combination and counter techniques)

As with standing work (tachi waza, see page 71), combinations and counters can also be used in the groundwork element of judo. There is a huge variety of moves as judoka are constantly developing new ways to manipulate opponents in order to get them into a hold or to gain a submission.

renzoku waza/renraku waza

Combinations in newaza (ground techniques), normally involve the tori achieving a hold or armlock while endeavouring to score the ippon, but starting to lose control during the course of the struggle. The tori has two choices in this situation: he or she can try to maintain control either by using the original technique again or by switching to another groundwork technique. Some examples of newaza combinations follow.

kesa gatame (scarf hold) into kata gatame (shoulder hold)

The tori has applied kesa gatame, but during the struggle, the uke manages to free the arm being held across the tori's chest and under the tori's armpit. The tori has a choice of trying to regain the arm or of pushing the elbow across the uke's face and locking his neck into the uke's tricep muscle to strengthen the hold. The tori then grasps his own hands.

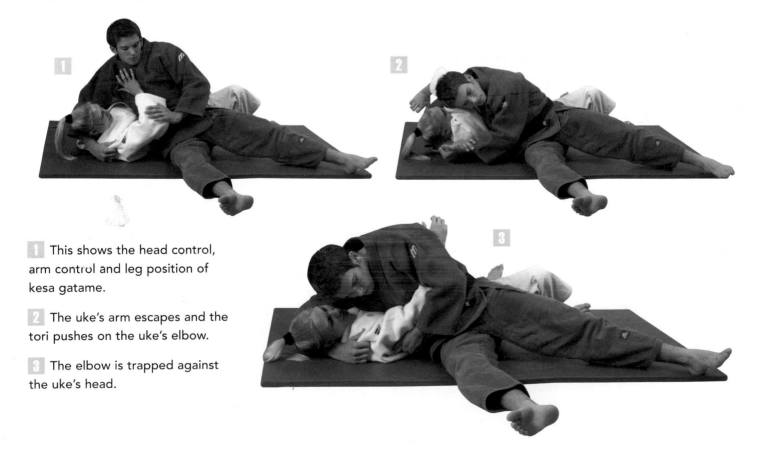

1 This shows the head control, arm control and leg position of kesa gatame.

2 The uke's arm escapes and the tori pushes on the uke's elbow.

3 The elbow is trapped against the uke's head.

kuzure kesa gatame (broken scarf hold) into ude garame (entangled armlock)

The uke is being held with kesa gatame. She has tried rolling the tori off, but he has countered with kuzare kesa gatame, taking his arm under her armpit. The uke uses her arm in an attempt to push the tori off. The tori releases the controlling arm and reaches across to her wrist. The tori's hand, which was under her armpit, grabs his own wrist and applies ude garame.

1 Demonstrating kuzure kesa gatame.

2 The uke attempts to escape.

3 The initial grip pattern required for ude garame.

4 This shows the application of ude garame.

kuzure kami shiho gatame (broken upper four-quarters hold) into ushiro kesa gatame (reverse scarf hold)

The uke is being pinned in the kami shiho gatame position. During the course of the struggle, the tori adapts to this, adjusting his under-the-shoulder grip to under the inside of her arm. He then swings the nearest leg to the uke's head under her shoulder, maintaining his grip of the uke's head.

1 Demonstrating kuzure kami shiho gatame.

2 This shows the step pattern required for the ushiro kesa gatame position.

3 Demonstrating ushiro kesa gatame.

kaeshi waza

Kaeshi waza are techniques that overcome an opponent's attack, in which the opponent is countered. As with standing techniques, it is also possible to make counter techniques in groundwork. Although the initial reaction is either to defend or escape, it is possible to set traps and/or create chances to counter an opponent's techniques. As with the tachi waza counters (see page 71), to save confusion in this section, 'the tori' is used to indicate the judoka who will be making the counter to become the dominant party. 'The uke' refers to the judoka being countered, despite his or her original attack.

kata juji jime (single cross strangle) countered by ashi gatame (leg armlock)

In groundwork, an opponent will attempt to apply this technique while facing the tori. Starting with the tori on his back and the uke in a chest-to-chest position, this strangle initially requires the uke's arm to become straight. The tori grabs one of the wrists, does not try to break the strangle, but manoeuvres himself onto his hip. At the same time, he takes the leg over the uke's arm. His ankle goes under the uke's chin, applying pressure to the arm – this is ashi gatame.

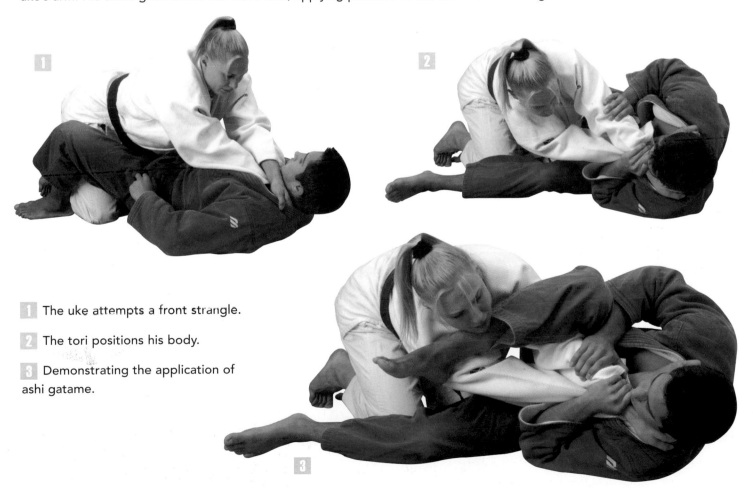

1 The uke attempts a front strangle.

2 The tori positions his body.

3 Demonstrating the application of ashi gatame.

yoko shiho gatame (side four-quarters hold) countered by kata te kata ashi jime (one-hand-one-leg strangle)

The tori is being held with yoko shiho gatame. During the struggle, he slips his hand under the uke's chin and grasps the furthest lapel, trying to get as deep as possible in order to get close to the carotid artery. The tori then lifts his leg as high as he can past the uke's leg and brings the back of the knee in contact with the side of the uke's neck. The thigh is in contact with the carotid area. The tori applies pressure with his hand and leg simultaneously to apply the strangle.

1 The uke holds the tori with yoko shiho gatame.

2 This shows the tori's hand placing for the strangle.

3 The tori applies kata ashi jime.

yoko shiho gatame (side four-quarters) countered by sangaku jime (triangle strangle)

The tori is being held with yoko shiho gatame. He grips the back of the uke's lapel with a thumb grip and uses the forearm to push against the uke's neck. At the same time, he swings his leg up, and, positioning the back of it against the uke's neck, he pushes down. The tori then places the back of the knee on the front of the upper part of the foot. The position of the legs means that the uke's head is trapped, as is one of the uke's arms. The squeezing action applies pressure to the carotid artery, ultimately achieving a submission.

1 The uke holds the tori with yoko shiho gatame.

2 The tori pushes the uke's head.

3 Demonstrating the first stage of the strangle.

4 The tori applies sangaku jime.

chapter three
tae kwon do

Tae kwon do is a Korean martial art that employs mainly kicking, punching, striking and evasive techniques. It has been developed from a unique historical and philosophical background. Tae kwon do developed from Korean martial arts that date back over five thousand years. The Korean peninsula was often unsettled by tribal warfare, as well as by incursions from neighbouring countries. During ancient times, both the Mongols and the Chinese Manchu Ch'ing dynasty invaded the Korean peninsula.

The Three Kingdoms period (40 BC to the 6th century AD) was a particularly important time for the development of Korean martial arts. As the name suggests, the Korean peninsula mainly comprised three kingdoms: Koguryo, Paekje and Silla. They were constantly fighting to gain control of the Korean peninsula and dominance over each other. Each kingdom had its own kings and tribal chiefs, and consequently its own military training systems. It is

through this constant rivalry that early Korean martial arts began to develop. Korean martial arts that developed in this era include subak (or taekkyon), sonbae, soobakhee, soobyuk, beekaksool, soobyukta and kwonbub.

The name 'tae kwon do' is composed of three parts. 'Tae' means 'foot', 'leg' or 'to step on'; 'kwon' means 'fist' or 'fight'; and 'do' means 'the way' or 'discipline'.

Modern tae kwon do refers to a fighting system developed by the Koreans over many years that uses the hands and feet to deliver high-energy impact techniques for survival in confrontational situations. These techniques take the form of punches, strikes, kicks and blocks. In any aggressive situation, the mind should remain peaceful and the martial artist should recognise that the true enemy may be his or her own aggression.

Today, the Korean martial art of tae kwon do shares similarities with many other Oriental martial arts. Countries surrounding Korea, such as Japan and China, have influenced the evolution of tae kwon do. Despite this evolutionary history, tae kwon do is very distinct from other Oriental martial arts.

Tae kwon do is dynamic in both its evolution and performance, and this dynamic nature is often reflected in the life and minds of Korean citizens.

Tae kwon do has now developed into an international sport and is recognised as such by the IOC (International Olympic Committee).

the philosophy of tae kwon do

Spiritual philosophies such as Taoism were vital to the inception of tae kwon do. Although much of tae kwon do training is based on traditional methods, nothing remains static, and tae kwon do continues to develop as further knowledge becomes integrated into the art.

To understand tae kwon do fully, it is necessary to examine the traditional Korean philosophy that has led to the development of tae kwon do. The philosophy known as Hongik-ingan describes actions that benefit the universal welfare of humankind. Jaese-ihwa, a philosophy that means 'divine rationalisation of human beings', became part of the Hongik-ingan philosophy during the Old Chosun Age. Hongik-ingan philosophy was represented by Seon philosophy in the Koguryo period. The Seon philosophy included ideals such as national pride and 'no retreat from fighting'. The Seon philosophy was incorporated into martial-arts training and was reflected in the Hwarangdo spirit during the Silla dynasty.

During the Silla-kingdom period, a book known as the Sesokokye was published that explained three characteristics of the Hwarangdo spirit. These characteristics were loyalty to your nation (Chung), filial piety to parents (Hyo) and trust (Shin). From these virtues, the five principles of the world (Sye-sok-oh-kye) and three virtuous conducts, or three kinds of beauty (Sam-mi), were formulated.

This philosophy became a basic way of life for the Hwarang, giving values and principles for living to those involved in martial-arts training. Tae kwon do spirit was inherited from the Hwarangdo spirit. This is evident from the five precepts of tae kwon do, which are etiquette, perseverance, modesty, self-control and indomitable spirit.

The five basic precepts of tae kwon do and the qualities that they represent can be described as follows.

Etiquette (Ye Ui): To respect your instructors and your fellow students; to respect the grade that the person has attained; to be polite; to respect everyone as an individual.

Perseverance (In Nae): With patience, goals can be achieved.

Modesty (Yom Chi): To have the ability to remove the ego and believe that you are equal to all other humans, irrespective of their background or experience. This especially applies to instructors and competition winners.

Self-control (Guk Gi): This includes self-control when sparring, as well as self-control in your everyday life.

Indomitable spirit (Baekjool Boolgool): To show courage when faced with a seemingly impossible situation; the ability to retain your fighting spirit.

philosophy of the Hwarang – the Sye-sok-oh-kye

1	Sa-kun-lee-chung	Loyalty to your country.
2	Sa-chin-lee-hyo	Honour and respect your parents.
3	Kyo-u-lee-shin	Trust and sincerity in friendship..
4	Lim-cheon-mu-t'wi	Never withdraw on the battlefield.
5	Sal-saeng-yu-taek	Justice; do not take another life without just cause.

the Sam-mi

1	modesty	Modesty refers to the spirit of contributing to social development rather than that of the self.
2	frugality	Frugality means not to waste.
3	Kyo-u-lee-shin	Restraint.

tao

Taoism is an important part of tae kwon do philosophy. It is very useful to have a grasp of the basic concepts of Taoism in order fully to understand the history and techniques used in tae kwon do.

Taoism is regarded as a Chinese concept, although the ideas of Taoism are ancient and spread throughout the Far East. It was common for an intellectual in the Far East to have read the 'Chinese classics'. This means that, among other things, they studied Taoism.

An understanding of Taoism helps you to understand the context within which the arts were invented and is a way of learning about another culture and way of life that can enrich your own lifestyle.

If you take a look at the Korean flag (above), you will instantly understand the emphasis and pride that the Koreans put on and have in their Taoist spirituality. The symbol in the middle is the yin–yang symbol, and the bars around the outside are trigrams from the Chinese oracle the I-Ching.

The first thing to understand is that Taoism is not a religion. Concepts such as the oneness of the universe are contemplated within Taoism, but no deity is worshipped, and there is no belief in a supernatural power that governs the universe.

Taoism comes from the observation of one's self in the universe and the interactions between the self and the universe. It is not as complicated as it sounds. For example, the seasons have an effect on us. When winter changes to spring, we feel changes inside ourselves. Without pre-judging whether it is good or bad, Taoists will notice these changes. Understanding how you are in the world that you live in gives you the chance to feel a part of it, rather than existing as a lone entity that is buffeted by seemingly chaotic forces.

Taoism is not a thing that can be handed over to another person. It is based on exercises in experience, rather than an intellectual exercise. After work and study, you gradually start to learn and integrate the concepts and theories.

yin and yang

The concept of yin and yang is worth studying by the serious martial artist – no matter what their style.

The symbol is a very clever piece of graphic design. Look at it for a while and think about what it may be telling you.

Let's start by looking at the colours, black and white. Black represents yin and white represents yang. The colour black is black because it absorbs light; conversely, the colour white reflects all frequencies of light and looks white to the eye.

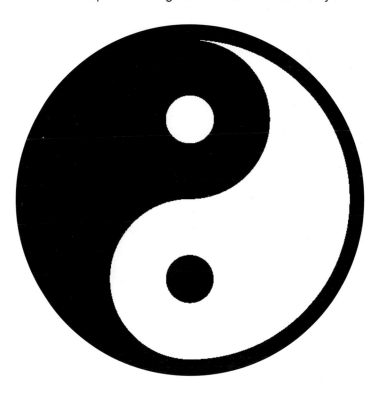

In yin and yang theory, yin is the receptive (it absorbs) and yang is the creative (it expands). The reflective white light represents the expansion of yang, and the contraction of yin is represented by the absorption of black.

So opposites can be described as being linked in pairs, such as life/death, hot/cold, up/down, in/out etc.

This leads us to the idea that one cannot exist without the other. How can you have everything in one colour? You would not need two or more colours because everything would be either black or white! The intermeshing of the two colours on the symbol represents this concept.

The circular shape of the symbol suggests that the co-existence between the entities of yin and yang is cyclical. Yin must follow the extreme of yang, just as yang must follow the extreme of yin. A good example of this is breathing. After breathing in (yin), the energy becomes yang, and you must breathe out.

There are many other concepts bound to the symbol, but the last one that we will discuss here is the dots in the halves of the symbol. This means that within yin there is yang, and within yang there is yin. An implication here is that yin and yang are not absolute; they are relative to each other.

If I have a flashlight that is brighter than yours, it gives out more energy, so it has more yang energy. If the sun comes out, then it has much more energy than my feeble flashlight, so my flashlight becomes yin, but it is still yang compared to your less bright one.

So how does this apply to martial arts? The more you think about it, the more you will find, but here are a few examples based on what we have already discussed.

The punch with the right hand is a yang motion, while the left hand is in a protective, yin position.

If you throw out your fist, it is a yang movement because it is expanding or moving away from your body. If you pull your hand back for a block, then the movement is coming towards you and is yin.

Now push your fist outward in a yang move. Repeat the movement.

To repeat the movement, you needed to pull your hand back before you could push it out again. In yin and yang terms, you used the yang energy when you pushed your fist out the first time, so you could not expand with another fist until you had

contracted and become more yin first. It would be like trying to breathe out twice in a row.

This is true in all martial arts – if you try to stay expanded or contracted all of the time, you will not be able to move; yin and yang must therefore follow one another in a cycle.

i-ching

In Taoism, there are no absolutes in yin and yang. If yang becomes extreme, it gradually becomes yin.

This idea gives rise to a view of the universe that can be described as a binary pattern of yin-and-yang combinations. This is the basic idea behind the I-Ching, or Book of Changes.

The theory of the I-Ching is connected to the Taoist idea of creation. From the original source, wu chi, come the two opposites – yin and yang. Yang and yin are represented by a solid line and a broken line:

—— ————
yang yin

This kind of binary representation has resonances with modern computer technology. Just as a binary word on a computer is made of an array of binary digits, the characters of the I-Ching are made in the same way.

If we add another line to the original, we will have four different possibilities or combinations.

The addition of another line gives us three lines, and the three lines are commonly called 'trigrams'. Adding another binary digit to the system will give us eight possibilities, or eight characters. Each trigram is attributed different qualities, such as heaven, earth, thunder etc. The attributes are based on the balance of yin and yang within the trigram. The trigram, which consists of yin and yang elements, is the fundamental building block for the I-Ching.

Grouping the trigrams together gives 8 x 8 = 64 possibilities. There are therefore 64 different hexagrams in the I-Ching or Book of Changes.

ki

According to the philosophies of the East, there is an energy field that transforms our bodies from being empty vessels to living entities. The Koreans and Japanese call this energy field 'ki', and the Chinese, 'chi', while Indian yogis call it 'prana'.

It is this same energy that a shiatsu (energy massage) practitioner or an acupuncturist will use to try to heal a patient or client. The theory states that if the ki in your body can flow evenly throughout your body, then you will be healthy. If the ki becomes blocked or cannot flow for some reason, however, then illness can set in.

The less well-known Korean method of using energy to heal is called 'amma'. It uses concepts from China and Japan and interprets them in a Korean way.

This kind of therapist will use his or her touch to try to distribute the flow of ki evenly. The acupuncturist will do the same with needles. Both techniques have become very popular in the West in recent years.

Healing and martial arts have been linked for many years because of this connection to ki. Many of the great masters also had a good understanding of energetic healing, or at least an instinctive feel for the subject.

The reason for this is that ki can be channelled and put to different uses. If you want to use it to heal, then your mind will be in a very different thought pattern to that if you wanted to hurt someone. In both instances, you will have projected your ki, but the intention of your mind rules the way that it works.

If you want a demonstration of ki, think about the tae kwon do student who breaks pieces of wood with his strikes. If you are hitting a piece of wood, you do not aim at the piece of wood, you aim through it.

If you aim at the wood, you will hurt your hand. If you aim through the wood, it will break. This is an example of using your intent to extend the ki. If you can develop sensitivity to ki, then your tae kwon do will change.

danjon

In traditional Korean medicine, the danjon is the name for the centre of your abdominal region. This is the area just below your navel. In traditional Chinese medicine, it is called the tan tien, and the Japanese name for the whole abdominal area is the hara.

In terms of tae kwon do, our danjon is the point through which all movement emanates. If you try to kick or punch using only an arm or leg, then your kicks and punches will be weak. If you can connect the movement to your danjon, then you will use the whole of your body and the technique will be powerful. In Korean thought, the danjon is one of the most important energy centres in the human body. Those who are trained to be sensitive in such things can use the danjon as a diagnostic area and can deduce physical or emotional problems in a person by touching or examining the danjon area

The therapist assesses and senses the ki of a person in the danjon, where all of the different energies in the body meet. By touching a specific area, it is possible to determine the state of those energies.

Your danjon is like a second brain. We already know this in a way, and it is reflected in our language: we have all had a 'gut reaction' to a situation.

Practising meditation will increase your sense of your danjon, and your 'second brain' in the danjon will communicate better. This is really a non-intellectual type of communication, but it is also very intuitive.

We all know what it is like when trying to use logic to decide what to do in a situation. We weigh up the pros and cons and then usually decide to go with what our 'gut reaction' told us to do in the first place.

If you can develop your sense of danjon, you can side-step the weighing-up bit and go straight for the action.

In a fighting situation, this means that you will be able to react without having to weigh up the process in your thinking mind. This will make you much faster and more accurate – both useful tricks for tae kwon do!

is it for me?

Is tae kwon do suitable for you? If you want to do it, then yes, it is. All you need is the motivation to begin, and the driving force behind that motivation will vary from person to person.

The tae kwon do student will benefit from increased physical fitness and psychological well-being. Physically, the student will improve in stamina, strength, flexibility, balance and control. Psychologically, tae kwon do is known to reduce tension, depression, anger, fatigue and confusion and to increase mental vigour in both male and female participants (Toscovic, 2001). Additionally, tae kwon do has been shown to improve leadership skills (Kurian, 1993).

There is no minimum age when a student can begin studying tae kwon do. Tae kwon do can be an ideal sport for children as it will teach them discipline and self-confidence, backed up with fitness training.

Speak with the class instructor before taking a young child to train. If the instructor considers that your child is mature enough, then give it a go. Check that the instructor understands that the child's body hasn't finished growing yet. For this reason, some of the harder stretches and conditioning exercises (such as knuckle press-ups) should be left until they are older.

There are no age limits in tae kwon do. Even so, older people should speak to their doctor to assess their fitness before starting tae kwon do. There are very few medical conditions that completely exclude you from training. If you can devise a plan with your instructor and your doctor, you should be alright. Indeed, recent research (Brudnak et al, 2001) shows that through tae kwon do, elderly students can increase the number of press-ups that they can perform, and improve their trunk flexion and balance time on each foot. The presence of older people in a club is often positive as their maturity may influence some of the younger students.

what do I need?

When you first enter the dojang or training hall, most instructors will allow the student to train in tracksuit bottoms and a T-shirt. Tae kwon do is usually done barefoot, so this saves on the cost of footwear!

When you have decided that tae kwon do is for you, then you will be expected to buy a dobok. The dobok is the traditional outfit worn for training in many martial arts. The tae kwon do dobok tends to be made from a lighter material than the judo gi because it is less likely to be torn. The cost of a basic dobok will usually start at around £15.

After a while, your instructor will start to teach you kyorugi, or sparring. If you intend to practise sparring, it is sensible to invest in protective equipment. Try to buy the best-quality equipment that you can afford as it will work better and last longer than cheaper equivalents.

There are many types of body armour and head protectors available. Some tae kwon do associations do not use any at all, however, and your instructor will advise you if you need to buy them. If it is essential, the club will usually have items available to borrow.

Your club will usually possess such items as kicking paddles, focus mitts, body armour and head protection, although there is nothing to stop you from buying your own if you really get bitten by the bug.

1	Gum shield (white or translucent)	Costs a lot less than getting your teeth fixed. Buy a good one that will not slip out of your mouth. Consult your dentist if in doubt about the quality.
2	Groin protector	Well, we don't really need to say much about that! Buy a proper martial-arts groin protector, not the 'cricket-box' type, as it will give better protection. Ladies should not forget this piece of equipment either. The further it extends into your abdominal region without limiting your movement, the better.
3	Bust protector	Obviously for the ladies.
4	Head guard	Protects the sides and top of the head.
5	Body protector or hogu	Protects the chest and stomach.
6	Forearm protector	Prevents bruising to the forearm.
7	Shin protector	Note that shin bruises are very common tae kwon do injuries.

belts and grades

When you go to your first tae kwon do class, you will see the tae kwon do students arranged in neat lines. The ones at the front will have black belts, and those at the back, white belts. Students in the middle will have various-coloured belts.

The colours of their belts will tell you the level of training that the tae kwon do students have reached through their gradings.

The belts are awarded in a hierarchical sequence that always starts with a white belt and finishes with a black belt. The intermediate belts represent the grades of the intermediate tae kwon do students.

Shown at right are the belt colours, ranging from white to black, for tae kwon do.

Attaining the grade of black belt is a great achievement in tae kwon do.

level	grade	
10th kup		white
9th kup		yellow tag on white belt
8th kup		yellow belt
7th kup		yellow belt with green tag
6th kup		green belt
5th kup		green belt with blue tag
4th kup		blue belt
3rd kup		blue belt with red tag
2nd kup		red
1st kup		red with black tag
1st dan		black

The word 'kup' means grades away from the black belt (dan). The 8th kup, for example, means that the tae kwon do student has eight more full gradings before he or she reaches the coveted black belt.

When you reach the black belt, it does not stop there! Many say that it has just started. There are various levels of black belt, called 'dan grades', starting at 1st dan and progressing to 10th dan. A stripe on the end of the black belt sometimes denotes the level of the black belt.

The skill level of the tae kwon do movements required for gradings depend on the grade of the student. In gradings, you will be required to perform the last poomsae that you have learnt, and possibly some previous ones. Movements applicable to the skill level of the student will be inspected. The 10th kup is not expected to show any kyorugi (or sparring). Higher kup grades will be required to perform kyorugi, however.

dojang etiquette

When you enter or leave a tae kwon do dojang, you should always bow. It does not matter whether it is a purpose-built dojang or the local village hall – for the tae kwon do lesson, it is all the same thing. Even if you just have to make a visit to the bathroom, you should always bow on the way out and on the way back in.

At the beginning and end of your class, you will perform the standing bow to the instructor. Before training with a partner, you should bow. When you have finished training with that partner, you should bow again. If you are going to train with another partner, you should do the same.

The bow is a sign of respect. When you enter or leave the dojang, it is a sign that you have respect for the dojang. When you bow to the instructor, you are not bowing to show subservience to the person in front of you. You are bowing to show respect for the person, what he or she has done in the pursuit of tae kwon do knowledge and all that has gone before him or her.

When you bow to your training partner, you are showing your partner respect and gratitude for the chance to train with that person, whoever they are.

With the bow should be a sense of openness and respect. It is nothing at all to do with your ego or the ego of the person that you are bowing to. If you subtract the respect element from martial arts, you remove one of the most valuable lessons that martial arts have to teach – both to individuals and to the world at large!

Other general rules include: do not eat or smoke in the dojang; keep your dobok clean and wear it properly; and always respect the instructor and your fellow students without prejudice.

Etiquette is an important aspect of tae kwon do philosophy and should continue in everyday life

the bow (kunyeh)

The bow should always be done with a sense of respect and humility – never just for the sake of it.

1 At ease – shui.

2 Move your heels together into the attention stance (charyot seogi), with your arms flat at your sides, body upright and your head held high.

3 Bend from the hips to an angle of around 30 degrees.

4 After one second in the bowing position, straighten your body back into the attention position.

5 Jumbi seogi.

stances and stepping

One of the most important aspects of martial-arts training, whether it is in tae kwon do or any other style, is the footwork. If your footwork is not good, then you need to work on it. No successful martial artist ever considered footwork to be unimportant.

Imagine a cannon on a ship or castle. When a cannonball is fired, the force from the explosion causes the cannon to move backwards if it is not held down. This is one of the principles upon which tae kwon do stances are based. If you fire out your fist like a cannonball and your feet slide backwards from the force, you have lost some of the impact energy.

If the punch makes contact, then the backwards reaction will be greater. If the reaction force knocks you off balance or throws you back, you will be in a more vulnerable position than before you threw the punch.

The solution is to use a good, strong stance that can withstand the impact of the reaction to your techniques. The stances in tae kwon do are similar to those in many martial arts.

Once you have learned how to use steady stances, think about how to move in a stance. If you are rooted to the spot, you will not be much of a martial artist. When stepping, and therefore in transition between the stances, you should try to be well balanced.

Stepping and stance training is the key to distancing yourself from the attacker. If you are good with your footwork, it is possible to put a person off balance just by stepping towards him or her in the correct way. Clearly, correct footwork is an aspect of the art that will be refined throughout your progression. The way that you understand your footwork in a year's time should be different to your comprehension at the present moment.

ready stance – jumbi seogi

The jumbi stance is used at the beginning of a class after the bow made to the instructor. It is also used at the beginning of all taegeuk poomsae and other formal exercises.

Your body should be straight and in good alignment. This shows that you have strong spirit. Stay alert when in the stance. If you allow your mind to drift when in the stance before performing poomsae at a grading, for example, your instructor will notice. You will have made your first mistake before actually doing anything. Tae kwon do is as much about state of mind as body!

Jumbi seogi is a neutral stance that is neither aggressive nor retreating. Your feet should be a shoulder-width apart, held parallel and pointing forwards. Your body weight should be evenly distributed between both feet.

We will now look at how to get into jumbi from the attention stance.

1 Stand to attention, with your arms at the sides of your body and your feet together.

2 Raise your forearms in front of your body, with your hands held as fists, palms facing upwards. As you are raising your fists, step with your left foot to shoulder-width and lower your arms to the correct position.

horse-riding stance – joochoom seogi

In this stance, you should look like somebody riding a horse, and not just from the position of the legs. Good riders make an effort to keep their backs straight, and this is essential in this stance.

The inner edges of your feet are parallel and approximately the length of two feet apart. You need to bend your knees slightly and direct your body weight inwards. Your weight should be distributed equally between your feet. Keep your shins in a vertical position.

This stance is really stable and is very useful for both attacks and defence. It can be very difficult for beginners because it is demanding on the muscles. Try standing in the posture for a few minutes a day to build up your strength.

walking stance – ap seogi

The walking stance is probably the most natural in the martial-arts spectrum. It is exactly what it says – the stance that we use for walking.

In the walking stance, your weight is higher than it is in the front stance, so it is more difficult to generate as much power. However, it has the advantage that it is more natural for the body. If you were in a potentially aggressive situation, then you could adopt a good walking stance without anybody noticing. This gives you the extra benefit that you can fall back on your training without being aggressive or obvious.

If you were to try to go into a long stance in normal life, you would not look natural and could antagonise a potential threat into becoming an actual threat.

In the walking stance, your feet should be a shoulder-width apart and pointing straight forwards. Your weight should be evenly distributed between both feet.

tiger stance – beom seogi

The tiger stance is so called because it is said to resemble the way that a tiger steps. A tiger will test the ground with its foot before putting weight on it. In the tiger stance, all of your weight is on the rear standing leg, while the ball of the leading foot gently touches the floor.

The main usage for this stance is when you suddenly need to move your body backwards in a defensive posture. If you step back in the tiger stance, your front leg is in an ideal position to deliver a front kick.

It is not usually a stance that is used for stepping in kyorugi (sparring), but some clubs may step in the tiger stance to train the legs.

Place your leading foot one foot's distance forward. Move your back foot to an angle 45 degrees to the front foot. The back leg supports the entire weight of your body. Your knees are kept bent, lowering the body. Your front foot is stretched so that only the ball of the foot rests on the floor.

front stance – apkubi seogi

The front stance is a strong, attacking stance that can also be used when blocking. The strength of the stance is in pushing your energy and strength forwards, hence its obvious application for attacking. It can also be used to make a retreat. If you are in a situation where you need to retreat, but also want to give a show of strength, you can step backwards in the front stance.

Your weight should be evenly distributed between both feet. The stance is around a shoulder-width wide and one-and-a-half shoulder-widths in length. Your front leg should be bent at the knee and your back leg, straight. Your hips should face forwards. Both feet should stay flat on the floor. Keep both of your feet facing forwards and parallel to each other.

stepping in front stance

To continue stepping, follow the sequence.

If you want to step backwards in the back stance, it is exactly the same. Just follow the instructions in reverse. The same pictures will apply.

When stepping, ensure that you move your feet forwards in a straight line. You can do this by imagining that your feet are moving along parallel railway lines.

Your head should remain at the same height. Achieve this by bending at the knees rather than straightening your legs as you move forwards.

1 Start in the ready stance (jumbi seogi).

2 Move your left leg forwards and bend your leg at the knee into the front stance.

3 Keep your left leg bent as you bring your right foot forwards. The foot travels forwards in a straight line. Keep your knees bent so that your head remains at a constant height. Be careful to keep your balance, and do not wobble.

4 Step forwards with your right foot in a straight line into the front stance. To continue stepping, repeat the sequence.

back stance – dwit kubi seogi

The back stance is primarily a defensive stance.

In this stance, two-thirds of the weight is placed on the back leg. The heels should be in line with each other. The front foot is straight, but this time, the back foot is at a 90-degree angle to the front foot. The front foot should be one step away from the back foot. The body is lowered slightly by bending both knees.

This stance places stress on the standing leg because it compresses all of the muscles in that leg. As you start to tire, be careful that you do not lean forwards and put too much weight on your front leg or allow the knee to collapse. Remember your tae kwon do spirit! After training, your muscles will become accustomed to the stance and it will not feel difficult.

The fact that most of your weight is on the rear leg means that you can quickly pick up the leading leg for a front kick. This is a useful trick that can change your retreat into an attack. It also puts you in a good position to power forwards from your rear leg into an attacking front stance.

Stepping in the back stance

1 Start in the ready stance.

2 Open your right foot to a 90-degree angle as you bend both knees.

3 Move your left foot forwards in line with your right heel.

As with the front stance, remember to keep your head at the same height and don't allow it to move up and down as you are stepping forwards.

4 Move your right foot close to your left foot. Turn your left foot through a 90-degree angle.

5 Step forwards with your right foot.

basic techniques

Basic techniques are the foundation of the martial art of tae kwon do. The only way to learn them is through repetition, until the technique becomes a natural movement.

Tae kwon do techniques are used either to strike an opponent or to evade a strike. When your understanding becomes deeper, you will learn that blocks can be used as strikes and vice versa. Some of the basic techniques can also be used as locks or throws. For now, we will look at a single application for each technique. Always try to think of new applications for the techniques as this will improve your tae kwon do and help you learn more effectively.

Repetition and practice will make your basic techniques strong and accurate. Basic techniques are the building blocks of tae kwon do. It is of little use if you know lots of different poomsae (routines), but are unable to punch your way out of a paper bag. A good technique can be used for poomsae, sparring and self-defence training.

Above: The punch making contact with a vital point – the solar plexus.

Below left: Making contact with the large knuckles of the fist maximises the striking power of the punch.

striking areas

If you go into a martial-arts shop, the chances are that you will see some kind of poster that illustrates the 'vital points' that you need for tae kwon do. These points are usually at acupuncture points called 'kup-so'. Frequently, a point will also be on a place that common sense tells you to protect, such as the ear or the eye.

The idea of these vital points is that they are targets for you to aim your strikes at. Frequently, there will also be a description of the best way to hit that point.

These charts are generally for the highly advanced student. For example, there are hundreds of points around the head and neck. If you get a good strike to the area with something like a reverse knife-hand strike, it matters very little which one you have hit.

There is also an idea that if your technique is good and your intention powerful, it matters very little where you hit the opponent, but how you hit them is critical. Again, this is a more advanced concept in tae kwon do.

For those who want to know more about the points and how to use them, a shiatsu book is a good place to start.

Many techniques can be used to strike the vital areas, for example, the punch can be used to attack the solar plexus. Similarly, the solar plexus can be attacked using a spear-finger thrust or a kicking technique. The technique that you use to strike the vital areas depends on many factors, such as the attacker's position or stance, his or her attack (whether it is a kick or a punch), the distance from the attacker, the techniques that you prefer to use and the vital areas that the attacker has left vulnerable to your strike. One of the most important skills that a martial artist will develop is the ability quickly to assess easy target areas on the opponent.

attacking techniques (kongkyok kisul)

punching (jireugi)

Everybody knows how to punch! Well, that is what a lot of people think at first. You just clench your fist and let rip! But along with that instinctive knowledge, we also know that some people are better at punching than others.

In tae kwon do, the mechanics of the punch are examined in fine detail. We find that what starts off as a basic movement that everybody understands can be refined to a high level. Which part of the hand do you punch with? Where do you punch? Where does the power come from? What range does the punch have?

These are all questions that tae kwon do students must be able to answer about their punches. But remember: no amount of understanding and analysis with the mind can replace practice! It is also worth noting that in the WTF style of full-contact sparring, punching to the head is an illegal attack.

Points to remember about punching	
1	Punches travel in a straight line from the waist to the target.
2	There should always be a reaction hand for the punch – that is, you pull one hand back as you punch with the other.
3	Sink your hips every time that you strike.
4	Exhale on the punch.
5	The fist twists at the end of the punch to increase power.
6	The elbow is bent at the beginning of the punch, but straightens at the end. This adds power to the punch.
7	Timing is crucial.
8	The power of the punch can be increased by moving the body forwards.

making a fist (jumeok)

Making a fist is probably one of the most basic of human reactions. If you are on a roller-coaster ride, when the carriage suddenly shoots down one of the slopes, the chances are that you will have made a fist. It's also likely that the fist has been formed correctly.

Sometimes, when you over-analyse things, they can get mixed up. If you are working from a pure gut reaction, as you are when the roller coaster is tumbling downwards, your mind has not confused things by analysing exactly which is the best way to place your fingers.

Some strikes will use specialised fists with a protruding knuckle, but these fists are not within the scope of this basic tae kwon do section.

1. Open your hand.

2. Bend your fingers.

3. Tuck your fingers tightly into your palm.

4. Fold your thumb over tightly – remember to keep your thumb tight as it is easy to catch and break your thumb when sparring if it is not kept out of the way.

The strike area is the two largest knuckles. There should be a straight line between the two largest knuckles and your forearm.

Keep your wrist straight.

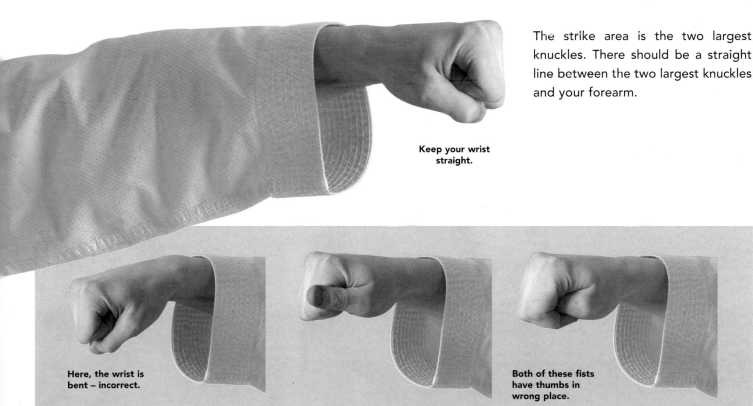

Here, the wrist is bent – incorrect.

Both of these fists have thumbs in wrong place.

straight punch – bandae jireugi

This punch is the basic building block of many of the other punches. It is fairly fast and has the power to stop an opponent. It is versatile and can be used on any target.

The most difficult parts of this punch are timing the left hand with the right hand (both should move at the same speed) and getting the twist at the end of the punch.

The punch is shown here in the ready stance. If it were done in the front stance, it would become another punch. It could also be done in the back stance.

Punches can be classified according to the height of the punch.

1	Contact area	two front knuckles
2	Range	medium to long
3	Target area	anywhere!
4	Power	strong
5	Speed	medium to fast
6	Difficulty level	easy
7	Suitability for sparring	n/a

1 **Face punch** (olgul jireugi): the target area is the head.

2 **Body punch** (momtong jireugi): the target is the solar plexus.

3 **Low punch** (arae jireugi): the target area is the 'danjon' (the lower part of the abdomen).

stepping punch

If you step forward in the front stance while executing a straight punch, you will have done a stepping punch. This is used to get nearer to the opponent in order to hit him or her.

It is very powerful because it should have the whole of your body weight concentrated into a small striking area. It is not as fast as the jireugi (straight) punch because you need to step to perform it. As with all punches, timing is the key to power!

1	Contact area	two largest knuckles
2	Range	long
3	Target area	frequently mid-section, but can be used anywhere
4	Power	very strong: it has the weight of your body behind it
5	Speed	medium
6	Difficulty level	easy, but requires co-ordination of the arms and legs
7	Suitability for sparring	good

1 Start in the ready stance.

2 Raise your right arm as you step up with your left fist.

3 Step forward with your left leg into the front stance. Twist your body and pull back with your right arm as you punch with your left fist.

jabbing punch

Every boxer needs to develop a good jab. This is not because you will normally score a knockout blow with a jab, although this has happened. It is because a good, fast, powerful jab opens the way for a more powerful technique like a kick.

Some tournament fighters are very keen on the jab–jab–punch rhythm. In this, the two leading jabs are used to open the defences and the final punch is where he or she gets the score, so watch out for it! Remember that punches to the head are not permitted in the rules of the World Tae Kwon Do Federation (WTF).

The essence of the jab is the same as that performed by a boxer. Watch and learn from boxers on TV as they are normally best at it!

The jab is a very simple punch that is executed by an extension of the arm. Do not forget your waist rotation, as without it there is hardly any power. Note that the reaction hand is hardly used for the jabbing punch. Always remember your guard when punching.

1	Contact area	ideally two front knuckles, but the whole of the front fist is common in sparring
2	Range	short to medium
3	Target area	head
4	Power	least powerful, but can still have quite a sting!
5	Speed	medium to fast
6	Difficulty level	easy, but power must come from the waist
7	Suitability for sparring	good, but be careful when the tournament rules dictate that you cannot punch to the head

Remember that the jabbing punch is a fast technique, so remain light on your feet.

A variation of the jabbing punch is the stepping jabbing punch. The mechanics are the same, but you step forwards into the front stance as you throw the punch.

1 Start in a fight stance.

2 Extend your hand in front of you in a snapping motion. Keep your elbow pointing downwards and use the two largest knuckles to make contact.

striking – chigi

Tae kwon do has a wide variety of striking techniques, as well as punching techniques.

The aim in striking is to use one of your contact areas for attacking a strike area on your opponent. Many of the striking techniques come from the realm of unarmed combat rather than competition. For example, a high-powered knife-hand strike to the neck can easily result in permanent injury or even death!

The techniques are a valuable part of tae kwon do, however, and are vital ingredients in the tae kwon do 'spirit'. In your classes, they will be studied either in poomsae or in one-step sparring.

We shall examine both closed and open-handed strikes. The striking areas for the open hand can be either the edge of the hand, the fingertips or the heel of the palm.

Right: The striking techniques used in tae kwon do are very powerful and an important part of training.

knife-hand strike – sonnal mok chigi

Some techniques in tae kwon do are just too dangerous for free sparring. The knife-hand strikes usually fall into this category. In sparring, it is possible to make mistakes – as in anything else. A bad mistake with a knife-hand technique can result in a serious injury. It is also worth bearing this fact in mind if you ever need to use the technique to defend yourself.

The technique uses the edge of the hand as shown and lends itself to attacking the sides. The momentum comes from a circular motion that starts either behind your head or in front of the body.

The technique can be executed as either a stepping technique or a standing technique in any of the stances.

1	Contact area	the edge of the hand, on the little-finger side
2	Range	medium to long
3	Target area	the sides, usually the neck or temple
4	Power	high
5	Speed	medium–fast
6	Difficulty level	medium
7	Suitability for sparring	not suitable for free sparring

the back fist

The back fist does not pack the same amount of power as the reverse punch or front punch. However, it still has enough power to be used as a destructive technique.

It is used for short-to-middle-range attacks and can be used to unfold an attack from inside the opponent's guard.

The back fist can be used to strike the temple or jaw (olgul bakkat chigi) or the front of the face (apchigi). The only thing that really changes is the plane of attack. To attack the face, the fist moves vertically. To attack the temple, the fist moves close to horizontally.

1	Contact area	the back of the two front knuckles
2	Range	short to medium
3	Target area	temples or jaw
4	Power	medium
5	Speed	fast
6	Difficulty level	easy
7	Suitability for sparring	not good as it can be a dangerous technique

outer back fist strike (olgul bakkat chigi)

This technique is used to attack the temple or jaw.

1 Start in the ready stance. Note that the motion of this strike is similar to that of the outer block.

2 Move the palm of your left fist across your body, with your right arm extended.

3 Pull your right elbow back as you strike towards your opponent's temple with the back of your left fist.

face back fist (apchigi)

This technique is used to attack the front of the face.

1 Start in the ready stance.

2 Move your left fist into position, with the palm of your left hand facing downwards and your right arm extended.

3 The striking hand should now move straight forward, towards your target.

elbowing techniques – palkup

Most of the punching and striking techniques shown so far have been for medium- or long-range attacks. If your opponent comes inside that circle of attack, however, many of the attacks will be difficult for you to execute.

However, this does not mean that you are beaten! Your tae kwon do spirit should be stronger than that. In the inner circle, you will use your elbows and knees.

Elbow and knee attacks can be very powerful. In tae kwon do, they are not usually used for free sparring. Thai boxers will use their elbows and knees, but these fighters have usually undergone intense physical and mental conditioning to withstand the blows. Even then, it is not uncommon for injuries to happen in that environment.

There are several possible attacks with the elbow. We will have a look at some of the more common ones. They are usually semi-circular or stabbing techniques. The main difference between them is the direction in which they travel. They are all devastating!

upper elbow strike (palkup ollyo chigi)

The upper elbow strike follows very similar dynamics to an upper-cut punch. If it helps in the beginning, you can imagine this technique as punching with the elbow.

It uses the edge of the elbow to connect with the point of the opponent's chin.

If you can catapult the strike from your hips, you will add more power to the technique.

1	Contact area	the edge or point of the elbow
2	Range	close to medium
3	Target area	jaw or chin
4	Power	very high
5	Speed	medium–fast
6	Difficulty level	easy
7	Suitability for sparring	not suitable for free sparring

1 Ready stance.

2 Extend your left fist. Pull back your left fist as your right fist starts to travel forwards. Start to lift your right elbow.

3 Power your right elbow into a high finishing position as your left fist snaps to the waist. Finish in the front stance.

elbow strike
(palkup dollyo chigi)

This powerful technique could be aimed high, to the side of the head, or lower, to the sides of the body and the floating rib. This is the most common version of the elbow attack.

It uses very similar mechanics to those of the hooking punch.

The technique can be made even more devastating by placing the non-striking hand around the back of your attacker's head (known as palkup pyojeok chigi). This means that the full impact of the strike is absorbed by the target area.

1 Ready stance.

2 Extend your right hand. As you start to pull your right fist back, your left fist starts to make an arc. Continue the arc as though punching to your throat using a hooking punch.

3 Extend your left elbow as you pull your right hand back.

kicks – chagi

If you look at the cover of most martial-arts books and magazines, you will see a picture of somebody executing a kick. If you watch a martial-arts film, then the chances are that the exponent will be a 'kicker'. Indeed, some well-known martial-arts actors are renowned for their ability to execute high kicks on the film set.

The simple reason for this is that kicks look good. A well-executed kick has an aesthetic quality that hints at the power, balance and training that the martial artist has worked at.

But kicks are not just there to look good. In practical styles like tae kwon do, nothing is included for aesthetic reasons only. A good kick can be a fast and powerful attack that can cover a long range.

Look at the picture below. Here, one of the tae kwon do students is executing a forward punch. In terms of punching, this is the longest-range punch that there is. But look at the

Tae kwon do kicks are very powerful and can cover a long range.

kick (above). A simple front kick hits the target and leaves the punching fist in mid-air.

Now think about the power. Look at the muscles in your arm compared to the muscles in your leg. Most people have at least twice as many muscle in the leg as in the arm.

But a kick is not just about the legs. You should use the whole of your body to drive the power through on a kick. You need to understand what part of the foot you are kicking with and the target area that you can connect with.

The kicks here are some of the basic ones. Nearly all kicks can be performed as jumping kicks to give added range and height. Some styles kick with the leading leg for extra speed, and others do not.

Kicks are an important aspect of tae kwon do. They help you to develop poise and suppleness, and kicking for a few minutes provides good cardiovascular training – any tae kwon do student can vouch for that. However, do not be lured into thinking that tae kwon do is all about kicking. This is but one aspect of a varied art form.

front kick – apchagi

The front kick is fast, powerful and versatile. It can be aimed at either the stomach (middle section) or the chin (high section) in sparring, and can be aimed at the groin and legs in self-defence.

The power of the kick comes from the hip – not just from the flick from the knee. The knee is lifted quickly, and the ball of the foot is shot outwards in a whiplash type of motion. The foot should travel in a straight line towards the target. As you kick out with your foot, you simultaneously drive your hips forward to generate power. After the kick, it is important to bring your foot back as quickly as you fired it out. This means that your leg cannot be caught so easily.

In the kick, you must use your hips to power your leg. If you can do this, then you will develop great power with your kicks. Note that it is possible to carry out the front kick as a jumping kick.

1 Starting in the front stance, hold your fists to the sides of your body.

2 Lift your knee.

3 Snap the kick outwards from your knee and power it from your hips. Pull your foot back quickly.

1	**Contact area**	the ball of the foot
2	**Range**	long
3	**Target area**	groin, stomach or chin
4	**Power**	high
5	**Speed**	fast
6	**Difficulty level**	easy
7	**Suitability for sparring**	highly suitable for free sparring

turning kick – dollyo chagi

The turning kick is very popular in sparring, principally because of its high power and speed.

The path of the turning kick is circular, and the attack comes from the side. It is therefore common to try to use it as a high kick to the side of the head. In competition, it is also possible to score a point by kicking to the mid-section if the technique is clean and hits the target properly.

For the traditional turning kick, you will hit with the ball of the foot. This makes the kick very powerful, and this method is therefore sometimes used for breaking boards in demonstrations or gradings.

In sparring and competitions, it is more common to use the instep of the foot. This allows the tae kwon do student to use exactly the same technique, but in a slightly less destructive way. If somebody hits you with the instep, it will hurt – but not as much as if he or she used the ball of the foot.

To execute the turning kick, you must lift the knee of your kicking leg and pivot around on your supporting foot. The higher you lift your knee, the higher your kick will be. When you release the kick, power is transmitted from your hips. After the release, you should then quickly bring your foot back again.

Start in the fighting stance, with your left leg forward.

There is a reverse version of the turning kick, mom dollyo chagi. It is also possible to perform the turning kick as a jumping kick or as a jumping and spinning kick.

1	Contact area	the ball of the foot
2	Range	long
3	Target area	head
4	Power	high
5	Speed	fast
6	Difficulty level	medium
7	Suitability for sparring	highly suitable for free sparring

1 Start in the fighting stance.

2 Lift your knee high into the chamber position.

3 Rotate your hips so that your leg becomes parallel to the floor.

4 Snap your foot out and make contact with the ball of your foot for maximum impact.

5 Now return your foot to the chamber position.

6 Return your leg to the floor and assume the fighting stance.

blocking – makki

Tae kwon do attacks are very aggressive. The inner nature of the person should be peaceful, but the defending person will normally respond with an attack that is aggressive and powerful. In tae kwon do, you do not wait for the attacker to go away. You neutralise an attack and deal with it quickly. Remember that in a real situation, it is highly possible that there may be more than one attacker. You therefore have no time for finesse with the first one because the second one will be on you.

This means that you need a way to deflect or neutralise the attack. This will usually be done by blocking with the forearm, although it is possible to use other parts of the body, such as the palm of the hand or a foot, knee or elbow, to block an attack. Most of the blocks in tae kwon do are designed to hurt the opponent. If the blocking tools, such as the hands, forearm and knife hand, are sufficiently conditioned, they can damage the attacker when you perform the block. As such, blocks then become an offensive technique.

Remember that if you have good footwork, then it is better to avoid the attack. In sparring, you should try to use your footwork skills to dodge the attack, only resorting to blocking if you didn't move quickly enough. This is because if you block a powerful kick, then you are likely to damage your arm. Always consider what you will do after the block.

Blocks can be used to protect the high area (olgul), middle area (momtong) or low area (arae).

Having outlined the three body areas and other considerations, note that there is a wide range of blocks available to the tae kwon do student.

The high block is a powerful blocking technique that is used to protect the head.

low block – arae makki

This is probably the most basic tae kwon do block. For this reason, it is usually taught to the tae kwon do student very early in the training.

The block uses the outer forearm to strike the opponent's attack and knock it out of the way. You will often see this block done in the front stance. It can also be done in any of the other stances.

A typical application for this block would be to defend against a lower front kick. Do not get stuck with this idea. What is to stop you from using exactly the same technique as a lower hammer fist strike to the opponent's inside leg or groin?

When blocking, do not try to hit your opponent's fist or foot as it is too easy to miss that target. It is better to use the block against the opponent's forearm or lower leg – larger targets – which will ensure the successful application of the block.

The low block defends against a turning kick.

 Start in the ready stance.

2 Point your right fist downwards and raise your right fist to your ear at the same time as you start to step forwards.

3 Drive your right arm down and pull your left arm back as you step. Finish with a twist of the hips in the front stance, extending your right arm into the lower block. Your fist should finish just in front of your leg, not on the outside.

poomsae

Poomsae are a fixed sequence of movements intended to teach the basic principals of tae kwon do without the use of an opponent. From a technical viewpoint, tae kwon do is poomsae. Kyorugi (sparring) is the practical application of tae kwon do.

Tae kwon do students learn and practise attacking and defensive movements against an imaginary opponent using a series of movements. It is important that each movement is performed as it would be performed in reality. Constant repetition of the poomsae, or moves, conditions your body so that each movement will become effective if you should really need to defend yourself.

Poomsae enable students to increase their breathing control, flexibility, balance, strength and understanding of power application.

The taegeuk poomsae were established so that students could learn the basic philosophical principles of tae kwon do. Each poomsae has its own meaning, and the movements of each poomsae should reflect the meanings of each of the forms.

the patterns – poomsae

The steps for all of the taegeuk poomsae follow the same basic pattern (see below right). Phonetic symbols of the Korean alphabet are used to describe the position and direction of movement of the practitioner. The tae kwon do student starts at position Na and moves forwards (towards Ga) or backwards (towards Na) along a vertical line. Movements to the left of the starting point are indicated by Da, while movements to the right are indicated by Ra.

In all of the tae kwon do poomsae, the performer must execute each technique with realism, as though responding to an attack from an opponent. The head should always turn first to look at the imaginary opponent before performing the technique. The eyes should always pierce straight into the eyes of the opponent and not look downwards, onto the floor.

Da 3	Ga	Ra 3
Da 2		Ra 2
Da 1		Ra 1
	Na	

taegeuk il jang

Taegeuk il (one) jang represents the Kwae symbol of Keon and means heaven, light, creation and yang. This poomsae represents the force of creation by containing the most basic of tae kwon do movements composed to accommodate white-belt students. It consists largely of the walking stance (ap seogi), but involves a shift to the front stance (apkubi). Movements include the low block (arae makki), inside mid-section block (momtong makki), middle punch (momtong jireugi) and front kick (apchagi). These basic techniques are used throughout the practice of tae kwon do.

1 From the Na position, look towards Ga in the ready stance (kibon jumbi seogi).

2 Turn anti-clockwise to the left in the direction of Da 1, place your left foot along the line of Da 1 in a left walking stance (ap seogi) and simultaneously execute a low block (arae makki) with your left hand.

3 Step forward, place your right foot in the direction of Da 1 in a right walking stance (ap seogi) and execute a mid-section punch (momtong bandae jireugi) with your right hand.

4 Turn in a clockwise direction by pivoting on the ball of your left foot, place your right foot in the direction of Ra 1 in a right walking stance (ap seogi) and simultaneously execute a low block (arae makki) with your right hand.

5 Step forward in the direction of Ra 1 into a left walking stance (ap seogi) and execute a mid-section punch (momtong bandae jireugi) with your left hand. Place your right foot in the direction of Ra 1 in a right walking stance (ap seogi) and simultaneously execute a low block (arae makki) with your right hand.

6 Turn anti-clockwise by pivoting on the ball of your right foot, place your left foot in the direction of Ga in a left front stance (apkubi) and simultaneously execute a low block (arae makki) with your left hand.

7 Keeping your feet as they are, then immediately execute a mid-section reverse punch (momtong baro jireugi) with your right hand.

8 Turn in a clockwise direction, pivoting on the ball of your left foot, place your right foot on the line of Ra 2 in walking stance (ap seogi) and simultaneously execute a reverse inward mid-section block (momtong anmakki) with your left hand.

9 Step forward, place your left foot on the line of Ra2 in walking stance and deliver a mid-section reverse punch with your right hand.

10 Turn anti-clockwise and move your left foot in the direction of Da 2 in walking stance; now perform a reverse inward mid-section block using your right hand.

11 Step forward in the direction of Da 2 in walking stance (ap seogi) and deliver a mid-section reverse punch (momtong baro jireugi) with your left hand.

12 Turn clockwise and place your right foot in the direction of Ga in a right front stance and execute a low block (arae makki) with your right hand.

13 Keep your feet as they are and immediately execute a mid-section reverse punch (momtong baro jireugi) using your left hand.

14 Pivot in an anti-clockwise direction and step forward with your left foot to Da 3 in a walking stance; perform a high-section block with your left hand.

15 Execute a front kick (apchagi) with your right foot.

16 Place your foot towards Da 3 and execute a mid-section punch (momtong bandae jireugi) with your right hand.

17 Pivot clockwise on the ball of your left foot, face Ra 3 in walking stance (ap seogi) and execute a high block (olgul makki) with your right hand.

18 Deliver a front kick (apchagi) with your left foot and then position it in the direction of Ra 3 in walking stance (ap seogi).

19 Now execute a mid-section punch (momtong bandae jireugi) using your left hand.

Front view

20 Pivot clockwise on the ball of your right foot, place your left foot in the direction of Na in a left front stance and execute a low block with your left hand.

Front view

21 Step forward with your right foot in the direction of Na in front stance (apkubi) and execute a mid-section punch with your right hand with a loud 'kihap'.

22 Step forward with your right foot in the direction of Na in front stance (apkubi) and execute a mid-section punch with your right hand with a loud 'kihap'.

taegeuk yi jang

Taegeuk yi (two) jang represents the Kwae symbol of Tae, which means joy and signifies inner firmness and outer softness. Tae is feminine and is symbolised by the image of a lake, so it is not aggressive and is of a spiritually uplifting nature. This poomsae should be performed with ease and fluidity, but firmly, with control. This poomsae introduces punching towards the head of the opponent and the high block.

1 From the Na position, look towards Ga in ready stance (kibon jumbi seogi).

2 Turn anti-clockwise to the left towards Da 1, place your left foot along the line of Da 1 in a left walking stance (ap seogi) and simultaneously execute a low block (arae makki) with your left hand.

3 Step forward and place your right foot in the direction of Da 1 in a right front stance (apkubi). Execute a mid-section punch (momtong bandae jireugi) with your right hand.

4 Turn in a clockwise direction by pivoting on the ball of your left foot, place your right foot in the direction of Ra 1 in a right walking stance (ap seogi) and simultaneously execute a low block (arae makki) with your right hand.

5 Step forward in the direction of Ra 1 into a left front stance (apkubi) and execute a mid-section punch (momtong bandae jireugi) with your left hand.

6 Pivot anti-clockwise on the ball of your right foot, place your left foot one step forwards into a walking stance in the direction of Ga and execute a reverse inward mid-section block (momtong anmakki) with your right hand.

7 Step forward into a walking stance (ap seogi) in the direction of Ga and execute a reverse inward mid-section block (momtong anmakki) with your left hand.

8 Rotate anti-clockwise on the ball of your right foot and place your left foot in the direction of Da 2. Execute a low block (arae makki) with your left hand.

9 Step forward, place your right foot in the direction of Da 1 in a right front stance (apkubi) and execute a mid-section punch (momtong bandae jireugi) with your right hand.

10 Execute a punch to the head (olgul bandae jireugi) with your right hand.

11 Pivot clockwise on the ball of your left foot, place your right foot one step forwards in the direction of Ra 2 in a right walking stance (ap seogi) and make a low block (arae makki) with your right hand.

12 Perform a front kick (apchagi) with your left foot and place your foot one step forwards in the direction of Ra 2 in the front stance (apkubi).

13 Execute a punch to the head (olgul bandae jireugi) with your left hand.

14 Rotate anti-clockwise on the ball of your right foot, place your left foot in the direction of Ga in a left walking stance (apkubi) and perform a high block (olgul makki) with your left hand.

15 Step forward, place your left foot in the direction of Ga in a right walking stance (ap seogi) and perform a high block (olgul makki) with your right hand.

Front view

16 Rotate anti-clockwise on the ball of your right foot, take your left foot in the direction of Ra 3 in a right walking stance (ap seogi) and execute an inward middle block (momtong anmakki) with your right hand.

17 Move your right foot a little in the direction of Da 3, rotate clockwise on the ball of your left foot to face the direction of Da 3 and then execute an inward middle block (momtong anmakki) with your left hand.

18 Rotate anti-clockwise on the ball of your right foot, place your left foot in a left walking stance (ap seogi) facing the direction of Na and execute a low block (arae makki) with your left hand.

Front view   **Front view**   **Front view**

19 Execute a front kick (apchagi) with your right foot and place your foot one step forward in the direction of Na in a right walking stance (ap seogi).

20 Deliver a mid-section punch (momtong bandae jireugi) using your right hand.

21 Execute a front kick (apchagi) with your left foot and place your foot one step forward in the direction of Na in a left walking stance (ap seogi).

Front view   **Front view**   **Front view**

22 Deliver a mid-section punch (momtong bandae jireugi) with your left hand.

23 Execute a front kick (apchagi) with your right foot and then place your foot one step forward in the direction of Na in a right walking stance (ap seogi).

24 Deliver a mid-section punch (momtong bandae jireugi) with your right hand with a loud shout of 'kihap'.

25 End (keuman) by keeping your right foot at the Na position, rotate anti-clockwise on the ball of your right foot to face the direction of Ga and move your left foot into ready stance (kibon jumbi seogi).

kyorugi or sparring

One of the useful things about poomsae is that you can train on your own. You can work a little each day on the poomsae and ask your instructor to correct any imperfections.

Poomsae training on its own would be very one-dimensional and would certainly not reflect the true spirit of tae kwon do. To understand a technique, you need to practise it with somebody else. Practising tae kwon do with a partner is called 'kyorugi', which translates closely to the word 'sparring'.

Kyorugi is done on different levels. The first level involves three punches from an attacker. In this, the attacking person will make three steps.

The defender will respond by blocking each punch, and will deliver a counterattack on the final attack (three-punch kyorugi). This approach teaches tae kwon do students how to distance themselves and to become accustomed to the idea of an attacker.

One variation of attacking three times is for the attacker to deliver one single punch (one-punch kyorugi). In one-punch kyorugi, the attacker will counterattack immediately after the first attacking punch. The emphasis here is on power, speed and accuracy. You must be able to demonstrate that you are attacking the chosen target accurately, and are not simply aimlessly attacking.

The attacks and defences will be performed as though they are real, although there is no actual contact. The fact that both tae kwon do students understand the situation gives them the

chance to use full speed and power.

Sparring is also a form of kyorugi. Tae kwon do students try to attack each other to score points. This gives them the chance to test themselves against each other. It is an excellent technique for sharpening skills, and is the technique used for sport tae kwon do.

We will now examine some examples of sparring.

three-punch kyorugi

Three-punch kyorugi is often called 'three-step sparring'. This is the most basic form of kyorugi. Clubs train using different techniques in their syllabuses, but the basic concept is always the same. This training is a controlled way of blocking three punches from an attacker. Once the attacker has performed the last punch, the defender retaliates with a counterattack. Here is an example of three-punch kyorugi. This example should be useful for giving you the idea.

1 Start in the attention stance – charyot seogi.

2 Bow (kunyeh).

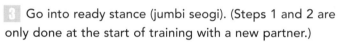

3 Go into ready stance (jumbi seogi). (Steps 1 and 2 are only done at the start of training with a new partner.)

4 In front stance, the attacker delivers a punch. The defender retreats into back stance and blocks using momtong makki.

5 The attacker delivers a second punch, while the defender steps back and blocks a second time.

6 The attacker steps forward and punches a third time, while the defender steps back and blocks a third time.

7 After the third block, the defender slides his right foot forwards into front stance and delivers a reverse punch (baro jireugi) with a loud 'kihap' (shout).

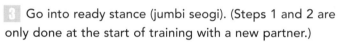

one-punch kyorugi

One-punch kyorugi is often called 'one-step sparring'. This is similar to three-punch kyorugi, except that the defender counterattacks after one punch rather than waiting for three punches.

If you are stuck for techniques, try using techniques in the poomsae. All of the techniques used in the poomsae are realistic and can be applied in a self-defence situation. It is always good to experiment – that way, you can make your own mistakes and learn in a more effective way. Always remember to perform the attack and counter-attack (defence) using both sides of the body. It is important to practise all techniques using both the left and right feet and hands.

example number 1

Defence using a foot sweep.

1 Start in the ready stance – jumbi seogi.

2 The attacker steps forward into a front stance and delivers a straight punch. The defender steps back into tiger stance and performs an inward block (momtong makki).

3 The defender rotates on the ball of his left foot and knocks the attacker's leg away.

4 As the attacker falls to the ground, the defender finishes the technique by punching at the head with a loud 'kihap' (shout).

example number 2 Defence by blocking using a kicking technique.

1 Start in the ready stance – jumbi seogi.

2 The defender anticipates the attack and so steps back into a fighting stance.

3 The defender blocks by using a crescent kick to the hand.

4 The defender then performs a side kick (yeop chagi) with a loud 'kihap' (shout).

5 The defender returns to a fighting stance.

example number 3

Close fighting defence using the palm, knee and elbow as weapons.

1 Start in the ready stance – jumbi seogi.

2 The defender blocks the attacker's punch by stepping forward and using a reverse knife-hand block.

3 The defender grabs the attacker's wrist and immediately strikes the attacker using a palm strike.

4 The defender continues by striking the stomach with a knee.

5 The defender finishes the technique by jumping and performing a downward elbow strike to the back with a loud 'kihap' (shout).

example number 4 Defence using a foot sweep and arm break.

1 Start in the ready stance (jumbi seogi).

2 The defender blocks the attack using a reverse block.

3 Immediately, the defender strikes the attacker's chin using an elbow strike.

4 The defender steps through with his left leg . . .

5 . . . and sweeps the attacker to the floor. Note that the defender is holding the attacker's arm with his right hand.

6 The defender punches the attacker with his left hand . . .

7 . . . and then grabs the attacker's arm with his right hand.

8 The defender breaks the attacker's arm using his shin as a lever . . .

9 . . . and continues the motion until the attacker is facing downward. Place your knee on his shoulder and pull back the attacker's hand so that he can't move his arm.

chapter four

kung fu

The history of kung fu goes back to primitive times, when tribes roamed the vast country of China. Their fight wasn't for trophies or medals, but for survival against wild animals and other tribes, or even within their own hierarchy (pecking order).

Martial arts began as a form of wrestling, imitating wild beasts. Participants would intertwine their arms to mimic the interlocking horns of animals, and the stronger would try to subdue the weaker. The only weapons that would have been available at this time would have been primitive clubs, sticks and small rocks.

As the tribes became more organised, so, too, did their combat skills, and through inter-tribal warfare they started to develop more sophisticated weapons. They sharpened the ends of sticks to make what are known today as spears. By tying a shaped rock to a club, they produced a weapon that we would recognise today as an axe.

There were also tribal dances used for festivals, or to prepare for war, where the actions of animals proved a great source of inspiration: for example, 'the courtship dance of the strutting peacock' or 'the war-like stamping and chest-beating of the great ape'. Furthermore, there are many ancient stories in Chinese mythology in which one creature comes to blows against another, such as a crane attacking a snake and an eagle attacking a bear.

One theory is that the Chinese tribes took inspiration from their dances and mythology in honing their combat skills.

Shang period (16–11 century BC)

As tribal societies developed, so, too, did their combat skills. The most dramatic change came during the Bronze Age in China, between the 16th and 11th centuries BC.

With the use of bronze, there was a huge advancement in the development of weapons, such as the battle axe, the halberd, the spear, the straight sword, the bow and arrow and the broad sword.

The tribal societies had, by this time, formed organised armies, which were well equipped with horses, armour and long-handled weapons like the long-handled broad sword (called the gwando).

Horsemanship skills improved to enable men to use their weapons more effectively.

spring and autumn and warring-states period (770–220 BC)

During this period, armed and unarmed combat skills became highly developed, with many methods of attack, defence and counterattack.

Martial-arts competitions became very popular, and, owing to a lack of protective clothing, many people were seriously wounded or killed. This did not stop the enthusiasm for competing, however.

Sword-fighting became very popular around this time, and many of the competitors were left with badly scarred faces and bodies.

This love of sword-fighting was shared by women, as well as men.

Qin dynasty (221–207 BC)

Competitions became much more strict during this period, with the enforcement of rules, the placement of referees and the development of the laitai (a raised open ring, pronounced 'lay tie'). So you not only had to learn the skill of combat, but also the skill of having to stay on the laitai.

During the periods previously mentioned, combat skills had been used to train the armies whose leaders were always struggling for supremacy. Many of the famous generals of the time were very skilled in armed and unarmed combat, and martial skills were constantly being refined or modified to keep up with the developing weaponry.

Numerous weapons were now being used, the most popular being known as the 'eighteen weapons' (the sword, longbow, crossbow, lance, battle axe, staff, long-bladed spear, cudgel, dagger axe, fork, truncheon, mallet, jingal, jointed bludgeon, chain, hooks, halberd and shield).

Han dynasty (206 BC–220 AD)
to Sui Tang dynasty (518–907 AD)

The development of martial arts within the military forces continued through the Han and Sui Tang dynasties. Officers had to take examinations so that they could be ranked by their skill. These examinations consisted of armed or unarmed combat, on foot or on horseback.

So now you can see how the Chinese martial arts developed through military training. Many students in the West have only heard the name 'kung fu' in relation to

Chinese martial arts, but, in fact, the correct term for all Chinese martial arts is 'wushu', which covers all aspects and styles of the Chinese martial arts.

The Chinese character Wu means 'military'.

The Chinese character for Shu  means 'art'.

Therefore, bringing the two characters together simply brings the concepts of military training and the arts together.

'Wushu' cannot be translated directly into English, but is generally known as 'Chinese martial arts'.

Song dynasty (960–1279 AD)

During the Song dynasty, martial-art associations were organised and set up in the different regions of China, with the art of kung fu/wushu being the most popular.

A section of the civilian population was now giving kung fu/wushu performances at festivals.

With many street performers showing their prowess by breaking large rocks with their bare hands and breaking spear shafts (being pressed to their throat), by far the most popular performance was that of taking on any and all challengers who wished to test their own skills.

Ming dynasty (1368–1644 AD)

During the Ming dynasty, practitioners of kung fu/wushu started to form many different schools.

Before this time, martial arts had mostly been passed down through word of mouth from master to student; there was very little written down as masters kept their own techniques secret from other schools or masters.

However, there are drawings that have been unearthed dating back to the primitive age that show men wrestling (shuai chiao) and in different combat stances.

Qing dynasty (1644–1911 AD)

During the Qing dynasty (1644–1911), the schools became more defined in their differing skills, each one developing its own approach to the many methods of training. There was also a rise in secret societies that used kung fu/wushu to great effect.

It is said that as students practised their art, they were taught poems or songs, the words of which held the secret of their fighting skills. Outside that particular school, therefore, nobody would know the meaning of the song or poem.

It was during this period that many of the styles that we know of today were developed, such as tan tui, xingyiquan, taijiquan, baghuaquan, changquan, bajiquan and tongbiquan.

In 1910, the Jing Wu Sports Society (Shanghai) was formed, and that was the beginning of the kung fu/wushu martial arts that we know today.

In 1928, the now famous Nanjing Academy (the Central Wushu Institute) was set up by the Chinese government to develop kung fu/wushu with a structured training syllabus, not just for self-defence, but also for the obvious health benefits that it affords.

Both the Jing Wu Sports Society and Nanjing Academy's main objective was to enhance the different schools of kung fu/wushu. They examined each movement and every posture in minute detail in order to identify the origins of each one. As a result, the kung fu/wushu school developed into an art form, with involvement from the top kung fu/wushu experts, who had many years of experience, which had been passed down through their respective families. These experts could correct postures and techniques, allowing the body to gain harmony through the movements.

Within the schools, through watching the students of various heights, weights and abilities practising, experts were also able to identify the attack and defence methods and to make improvements, thus making kung fu/wushu much more effective for each and every student.

These are the foundations of what we see in kung fu/wushu today. It has been said that a kung fu/wushu form looks like ballet combined with gymnastics. To be a ballerina, you need great strength and flexibility, while a gymnast requires tremendous agility. Combine these qualities with the attack and defence techniques of kung fu/wushu, and you have a martial art that is not only beautiful to watch, but also instils discipline, virtue and skill in each and every student.

Left: It was during the Qing dynasty that many of the styles known today were developed – including taijiquan.

kung fu schools

Tanglang

northern external schools – hard style

As kung fu/wushu developed, different systems became popular within their own provinces. There are well over a hundred different schools, and many more individual schools, within these groups. To give you some idea as to the differing styles, I have listed some of these at right. Unfortunately, there are just too many to list them all.

A generic term for these systems is: above the Yangtze river (Yellow River) northern style; chang quan.

Northern styles are characterised by speed and strength, with an emphasis on variations of footwork techniques and high and low kicks. Hence the expression 'northern leg'.

There are other schools, those of imitation boxing: hou quan (monkey boxing), zui quan (drunken boxing), ditang quan (tumbling boxing) and tanglang (praying-mantis boxing). All of these schools come under the generic term of 'external' schools.

shaolin quan	shaolin boxing
fanzi quan	wheeling boxing
zha quan	zha school of boxing
hwa quan	essence boxing
hua quan	flower boxing
pao quan	cannon boxing
hong quan	hong school of boxing
tonbi quan	full-arm boxing
mizong quan	maze boxing
liuhe	six-harmony boxing
tan tui	spring-leg boxing
chuo jiao	jabbing feet
baji quan	eight ultimate boxing
taizu chang quan	great-ancestor boxing
mian quan	silk-floss boxing

internal schools – soft style

Taijiquan is known as an 'internal' school of kung fu/wushu and has five major schools: chen, yang, wu, sun and wu/hao.

Chen school is the oldest known form, and this is a very powerful form of taijiquan that is becoming more popular in the West.

Yang style is the most popular form of taijiquan and was promoted by the Chinese government in the 1950s as a health exercise.

As stated above, there are also the wu, sun and hao styles. These are not so popular outside China.

Taijiquan is characterised by soft, light and slow exercise, which features continuously circling and fluent movements. The different schools of taijiquan stress the different aspects, hence the expressions 'soft' school or 'internal' styles.

Taijiquan is a very powerful martial art, and many of the old masters, who have gone down in history for their prowess within the fighting arts, have used this system.

The slow, focused and concentrated movements can be developed into very powerful postures for defence or attack, creating greater strength within the body.

southern internal schools – hard style

In provinces below the Yangtze river, the generic term is known as southern style or nanquan. Many of these schools originated in the Fujian and Guandong provinces and spread throughout southern China much later.

Southern schools are characterised by the powerful exertion of force, firm and steady footwork, clear-cut movements, strong positioning of the body to react to an attack from any direction and upper-body attack and defence, hence the expression 'southern fist'.

Nan Quan.

The most popular, and known as the 'five great schools', are:	
hongjia quan	hong school of boxing
liujia quan	liu school of boxing
ciajia quan	cai school of boxing
lijia quan	li school of boxing
mojia quan	mo school of boxing

There are many other schools:	
huhe shuang xing quan	tiger crane boxing
yong chuan quan	eternal-youth boxing
xia quan	knight boxing
hakka quan	hakka boxing
fojia quan	Buddhist boxing
baimei quan	white-eyebrow boxing
ru quan	Confucian boxing
nanji quan	southern-skills boxing
kunhan quan	kunlun boxing
kongmen quan	house of kong boxing
lianshou quan	han boxing

what is involved?

Within all major martial arts, there is a strict form of etiquette, a code of training and discipline. This stems from their military foundations.

salutation

Every school or style of martial art has a different salutation. For example, in the Japanese and Korean arts, the salutation is normally expressed with a bow of the head.

In Chinese kung fu/wushu, the salutation is usually demonstrated by the left hand covering the knuckles of the right fist, while holding the hands at chest height, in the centre of the body. Traditional styles of kung fu/wushu may have different salutations, however.

Whichever school of martial art it is that you are practising, the salutation is always performed when entering or leaving the training hall. It is also performed at the beginning and end of a class and at the beginning and end of a training or sparring session with your training partner.

The salutation shows respect for your training hall, your instructor and/or your training partner. The significance of the right fist covered by the left palm is that it shows that you will not use the fist in malice; it also shows the union of yin and yang – soft and hard.

Within the many traditional styles, the salutation may vary and be quite different to what I have explained above, but it will still be the training code for that particular style of kung fu/wushu.

The head instructor of the school would be addressed as 'sifu' (which means 'teacher'. In the old days, when the master only took on one or two students, 'sifu' meant 'second father').

clothing

You should always wear the uniform of the particular style that you are training in, and make an effort to keep yourself and your uniform clean and tidy.

Remove *all* jewellery and spectacles before you train. This is for your own safety.

Make sure that your fingernails and toenails are kept short and clean. This is necessary not only for your own safety, but for that of your partner as well.

If your hair is long, then it should be tied back.

can I do kung fu?

This is a question that I am frequently asked. It is essential to have realistic expectations. Although anyone can train in kung fu/wushu, it depends on what you are looking for in a class. To achieve a high level of skill will take time and dedication.

If fitness or self-defence is your aim, then almost any style would be alright, providing that you keep safety in mind.

If you like the idea of getting into the competition side, then you must choose a style or instructor that will give you the encouragement or incentive to follow this type of training.

However, as a potential student, note that training for competition is usually very challenging and different to, and much more demanding than, normal class training.

If you have, or have had, any medical conditions or injuries, you should consult your doctor for his or her permission before embarking on any form of training.

Then, if you are on any medication, or have any medical problems (this includes injuries, old or new), you should always inform your instructor and tell him or her if the medication changes.

what should I look for?

Check that the style is recognised by your country's governing body and obtain any information that it has. This should ensure that the school or style is reputable.

In England, the British Council for Chinese Martial Arts is the governing body, and this is recognised by the National Sports Council. In other countries, information on governing bodies should be available from that country's national sports council or committee.

You should always ask what qualifications the instructor has in the style that he or she is teaching. Also ask if he or she is insured and who his or her teacher is.

If you are able to, attend a class for an introductory session to see whether or not you like it. Note, however, that not all classes or instructors will allow this.

Get some background information on the styles that are taught in your area; this may help in deciding where to go. A rule of thumb is that if you like the instructor and what he or she is teaching, then stay with it, if not, find somewhere else.

Discipline is also something that you should be aware of. Some students may find this part challenging, but provided that the instructor knows his or her art, all good martial-arts schools will run disciplined classes or seminars.

kung fu stances

Within all martial arts there are stances; in kung fu/wushu, there are many.

The stances are the most important part of your basic training. If you do not have a strong foundation, your art will be weak, in the same way that a house without a good foundation will fall down.

Each stance is a component that defines your art; whether punching, kicking, blocking or sparring, your power must be generated from your stance.

Stances		
1	Forward-bow stance	(gong bu)
2	Riding-horse stance	(ma bu)
3	Empty-step stance	(xu bu)
4	Crouching-bow stance	(pu bu)
5	Scissor stance	(jian zi gu bu)
5a	Resting stance	(xie bu)
With stances 5 and 5a, the leg work is the same, but one stance is high and the other is low.		

It also helps to build up your upper and lower limbs and your eye, hand and foot co-ordination. If your stance is strong, then your art will be smooth, powerful and dynamic.

If your stance is weak, then your art will be unco-ordinated, loose and powerless.

Each school of kung fu/wushu may use stances in different ways: within the northern school, the stances are very low and wide, while in the southern school, they are not quite as low or as wide.

We will look at five basic stances that are found in all martial arts, although their names may differ.

1 forward-bow stance (gong bu)

high stance

1 Stand with your feet 15–20cm (6–8in) apart, fists on your hips.

2 Move your right foot forward (about 2½ lengths of your own foot). Bend your front knee, keeping your back leg straight. Bend the knee until your front thigh makes a 45-degree angle to the floor. Sink your weight through your front hip, not your knee. Your front foot should be in line with your back heel. Repeat the sequence on the other side.

low stance

Stand with your feet 15–20cm (6–8in) apart, fists on your hips. Move your left foot forward (about 3½ lengths of your own foot). Bend your front knee, keeping your back leg straight, until your front thigh is parallel with the floor. Sink through your front hip, not your knee. Your front foot should be in line with your back heel.

Repeat the sequence on the other side.

2 riding-horse stance (ma bu)

high stance

Standing with your feet together, move your left leg to the side to a distance of 2½ lengths of your foot. Your toes should point forwards and your fists should rest on your hips. Now bend your knees until your thighs are at a 45-degree angle to the floor.

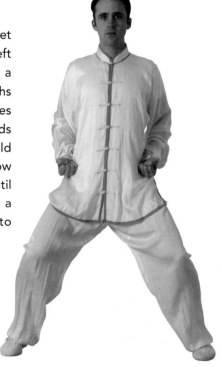

low stance

Standing with your feet together, move your left leg to the side by 3½ lengths of your foot. Your toes should point forwards, while your fists rest on your hips. Bend your knees so that your thighs are parallel to the floor.

3 empty-step stance (xu bu)

high stance

Stand with your feet 15–20cm (6–8in) apart. Move your left leg forwards by 2 lengths of your foot and sink your body weight into your rear leg. Your thigh should be at a 45-degree angle to the floor. Hold your hands in the 'on guard' position. Keep your back straight and your head erect.

low stance

Stand with your feet 15–20cm (6–8in) apart. Move your left leg forward by 2½ lengths of your foot and sink your body weight into your rear leg until your thigh is parallel to floor. You should be touching the floor with just the tip of your foot. Hold your hands in the 'on guard' position. Keep your back straight and head erect.

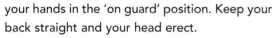

Repeat the sequence on the opposite side.

4 crouching-bow stance (pu bu)

high stance

Stand with your feet together. Slide your left leg out by 2½ lengths of your foot. Your thigh should be 45 degrees to the floor.

low stance

Stand with your feet together and slide your left leg out by 3½ lengths of your foot. Bend your right knee until your thigh is parallel to the floor. Push upwards with your right arm, palm facing upwards, and punch forward with your left fist. Keep your back straight, head erect. Repeat on the other side.

5 scissor stance (jian zi gu bu)

Stand with your feet a shoulder-width apart. Step across your right leg with your left leg. You should be facing forward on a slight diagonal. Sit down as far as possible onto your back leg, heel raised. Your back knee should sit in the hollow of your front knee. Keep your back straight and your head erect. Repeat on the other side.

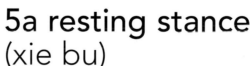

5a resting stance (xie bu)

Stand with your feet a shoulder-width apart. Step across your right leg with your left leg. Face forward on a slight diagonal. Sit on your back leg so that your buttocks are touching your calf. Your lower knee should not touch the floor. Keep your back straight and head erect. Repeat on the other side.

stance, fist and foot training

This is to build up co-ordination between the upper and lower limbs, as well as co-ordination of eye, hand and foot. This kind of training will build speed, power and flexibility.

Chinese kung fu/wushu has its own traditional training system. The exercises that follow are some of the fundamental training techniques for northern shaolin.

Fist and foot training are very important for co-ordinating the inside and outside activities. ('Inside activities' refers to the mind, whereas 'outside activities' refers to the bodily movements of the eye, hand and foot.)

The basic requirement of the body concerns posture and stance. When standing, the body should be erect and relaxed so that it can respond to an attack from any direction. The five body parts (head, two arms and two legs) should be well balanced in order to maintain co-ordination between the upper and lower limbs. The hand should co-ordinate with the foot, the shoulder with the hip, and the elbow with the knee. These are known as the three outside co-ordinations – wai san he.

Training in these fundamental techniques is the root of northern kung fu. If you practise on a regular basis, you will build strength, speed, agility and fluidity of movement.

riding-horse stance (ma bu)

exercise 1: thrust punch (chang quan)

1 Stand with your feet in riding-horse stance (ma bu). Clench your fists and rest them on your hips, with the 'heart' of the fist facing upwards.

2 Punch forward with your left fist ('eye' of the fist uppermost), turning your shoulder and hips as you go.

3 Withdraw your left fist, rotating it so that the 'heart' of the fist is facing upwards. At the same time, punch forward with your right fist, rotating it so that the 'eye' is facing upwards.

Make eight punches to the left, then eight to the right.

exercise 2: right and left bow stance (you zhou gong bu) and right and left thrust punch (you zhou chang quan)

This exercise increases the previous movement.

Practise this very slowly until you achieve co-ordination. Practise eight punches on each side.

1 Stand with your feet in riding-horse stance (ma bu). Clench upir fists and rest them on your hips ('heart' of the fist facing upwards).

2 As you punch forward with your left fist, turn your body to the right, turning your right foot out and sliding your left foot back into a 45-degree angle (into right bow stance – gong bu) as you thrust-punch (fist's 'eye' upwards). Focus your eyes on your punching hand.

3 As you withdraw your left fist, rotate so that the 'heart' of your fist is facing upwards. At the same time, turn your body back into riding-horse stance (ma bu), drawing your right foot back.

4 Return to the riding-horse stance (ma bu).

5 Repeat this movement on the opposite side.

Important points

1	You can practise this in either high or low stance.
2	You are turning your body to a 90-degree angle; keep your back straight and head erect.
3	Focus eyes on punching hand.
4	Ensure that your bow stance is strong and beware of your knee extending past the toes.

front snap kick (che chuai)

exercise 4

1 Stand with your feet a shoulder-width apart. This is the spring leg kick (tan tui).

2 Sink your body weight onto your left leg so that your right leg is 'empty', with just your toes touching the floor (empty step – xu bu). Keep your fists on your hips.

3 Raise your right knee as high as you can.

4 Kick your right foot forward, toes pointing forwards, and sink more of your body weight onto your left leg. Keep your balance and transfer the

Points to remember	
1	When kicking, hold your balance.
2	Do not lean back as you kick.
3	Do not kick higher than waist level.
4	Practise slowly to build up the power in your legs.
5	Only sink as low as is comfortable for you in empty-step stance.
6	Check that you feel the muscles in your thigh working.
7	If you feel discomfort in your knee joint, check your stance.

power into your right kick.

5 Bring the lower part of your right leg back down so that your knee is raised as high as it will go.

6 Then lower your right foot to the floor and centre your balance, standing back with both feet a shoulder-width apart.

Repeat on the other side, executing eight each time.

If you want to change the working muscle groups in your leg while kicking, all you have to do is pull your toes back and kick with your heel.

There is also a much stronger stretch in the calf muscle – a kick called heel kick, or deng tui.

hand and foot techniques – northern style

Within the northern and southern styles, the striking and kicking techniques vary considerably. These techniques are for reference, so that you can see some of the movements in northern kung fu/wushu.

But if you want to practise these techniques, they will help to co-ordinate your upper and lower limbs and your eye, hand and foot. Your shoulders will co-ordinate with your hips, your elbows with your knees, and your hands with your feet. The northern schools have a striking range that is normally a much longer range. The striking is based on the fist, the palm and the hook.

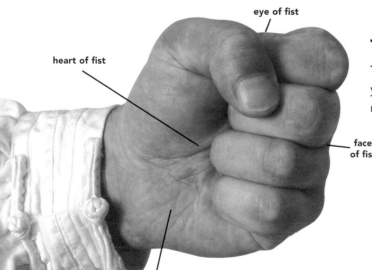

eye of fist

heart of fist

face of fist

heel of fist

fist (quan)

Tightly clench your fist, with the knuckles held evenly. Place your thumb across the mid-section of your index finger and middle finger.

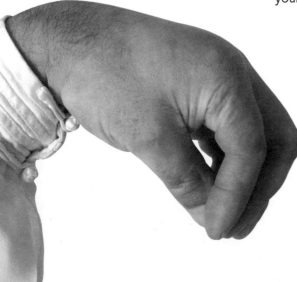

palm (zhang)

Hold your fingers together and straight, keeping your palm flat. Tuck your thumb into the side of your palm.

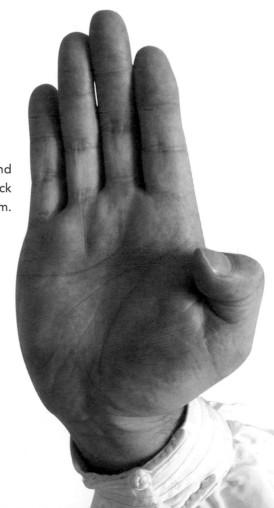

hook (gou)

Flex your hand at the wrist, with all four of your fingers touching your thumb.

fist techniques (quan fa)

thrust punch (chong quan)

As you move forward into the right bow stance (you gong bu), rotate your fist forward in line with your shoulders. The 'face' of your fist's knuckles should be even, and the 'eye' of your fist uppermost. Apply power to the 'face' of your fist. Practise the movement eight times on each side.

straight-arm chop (pi quan)

Circle your right fist over the top of your head, finishing in line with your shoulder. Apply power to the bottom of your fist. Circle your left palm above your head, with the palm facing upwards. Bring your feet together (bing bu). Practise the movement eight times on each side.

uppercut (liao quan)

From the riding-horse stance (ma bu), push your left forearm out in front of you, parallel to your chest. Sweep your left forearm down to knee level and then up, in line with your left shoulder. Turn your body into the left bow stance (zhou gong bu) and circle your right fist upward to shoulder level ('eye' of the fist uppermost). Apply power the 'eye' of the fist. Practise the movement eight times on each side.

hammer strike (za quan)

1 Raise your right fist above your head, then raise the knee on the same side up to hip height.

2 Smash the back of your fist downwards, into your other palm, with power applied to the back of the fist. At the same time, stamp your foot on the ground.

Practise the movement eight times on each side.

palm techniques (zhang fa)

push palm (tui zhang)

Step forward into the left bow stance (zhou gong bu), with your left palm striking forward, from your hip to level with your shoulder. Keep your fingers together and your thumb tucked into the side of your palm. Practise the movement eight times on each side.

palm chop (qie zhang)

Sit down in a right crouching-bow stance (you pu bu) and bring your right fist in to the hip of the bent thigh. Stretch out your left arm in line with your left leg, with the palm edge facing outward. Apply power to the outer edge of the palm. Practise the movement eight times on each side.

elbow parry (ger zhou)

In the riding-horse stance (ma bu), bring your forearm in front of your body, fist level with your chest and elbow slightly bent. Apply power to the forearm. Practise the movement eight times on each side.

hook elbow (pan zhou)

In the forward right bow stance (you gong bu), and with an outstretched arm, bend your elbow in front of your body at a 90-degree angle. Apply power to the front part of your forearm. Practise the movement eight times on each side.

leg techniques (tui fa)

front kick

Stand with your feet 15–20cm (6–8in) apart, with your fists on your hips, 'heart' of the fist uppermost. Raise your right knee as high as it will go and kick forwards, with your toes pointing forwards. To build up balance and strength, focus the power through your toes. Hold for a slow count of five and repeat on the other side. Practise the movement eight times on each side.

front snap heel kick (deng tui)

Stand with your feet 15–20cm (6–8in) apart, with your fists on your hips, 'heart' of the fist uppermost. Raise your right knee as high as it will go and kick forwards, pulling your toes back. Apply power through the heel of the foot. Repeat on the opposite side. Then practise the movement eight times on each side.

spring leg kick (tan tui)

Stand with your feet a shoulder-width apart. Sinking your body weight into your rear leg, bring the other leg up so that your thigh is level with your hip. Snap the leg out in front of you, with your toes pointing forwards. Apply power to the toes. Practise the movement eight times on each side.

hand and foot techniques – southern style

There are many more southern-style hand techniques – hand and arm (bridge) techniques – than in the northern style, hence the expression 'southern fist'. Southern styles are famous for their dynamic (bridge) training techniques, as will be described.

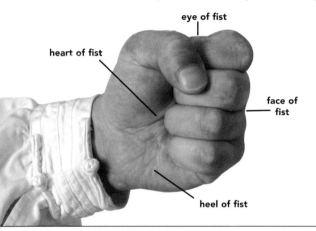

eye of fist

heart of fist

face of fist

heel of fist

fist (quan)
Hold your fist tightly clenched, with the knuckles held evenly. Place your thumb across the mid-section of your index finger and middle finger.

palm (zhang)
Hold your fingers together and straight, keeping the palm flat. Tuck your thumb into the side of your palm.

1 hook (gou)
Flex your hand at the wrist, with all four fingers touching your thumb.

2 tiger paw (hu zhao)
Spread your fingers and hook the second and third joints of your fingers, and the second joint of your thumb, so that your palm is exposed. Your hand should be flexed back slightly.

3 eagle claw (ying zhao)
Open your hand fully, then hook your fingers at the first joint. Draw your thumb back to the edge of your palm. Keep your palm exposed and flex your wrist back slightly.

4 single finger (dang shi)
Flex your wrist back, with your index finger pointing upwards. Curl the other three fingers inwards and tuck your thumb into the side of your palm. This is to strengthen the forearm (bridge).

5 crane's bill (he zui shou)
Connect the tips of your four fingers and your thumb without flexing your wrist.

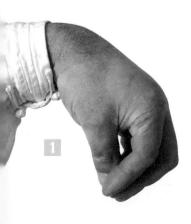

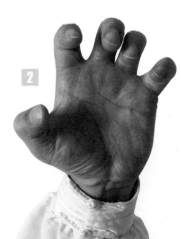

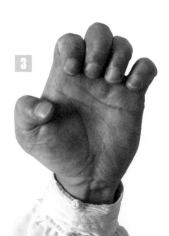

punching techniques (quan fa)

thrust punch (chong quan)

Step forward into the left bow stance (zhou gong bu), with your right fist at waist level. Punch forward with your right arm, rotating the 'eye' of the fist upwards and keeping the knuckles on the 'face' of the fist even. Raise your left palm to face your right forearm. Practise the movement eight times on each side.

tossing chop (pao quan)

Step forward into the left bow stance (zhou gong bu). Punch upwards with your left fist as you punch outwards with your right. Co-ordinate both arm movements. Focus power into the 'eye' of the fist.
Practise the movement eight times on each side.

covering strike (gai quan)

From the riding-horse stance (ma bu), turn into the left bow stance (zhou gong bu). Circle your right arm up, over your head, with your fist striking downwards. Focus power into the 'heart' of the fist. Practise the movement eight times on each side.

flail fist (bian quan)

Standing in empty-step stance (xu bu), move your arms across your body at shoulder height. Clench your right fist and hold your left palm by your right shoulder. Apply power to the back of the fist. Practise the movement eight times on each side.

palm techniques (zhang fa)

tilt palm (tiao zhang)

In riding-horse stance (ma bu), with your arms outstretched and palms at shoulder level, curve your palms in an outward movement. The power should move upwards and be applied to the fingers. Practise the movement eight times.

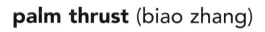

palm thrust (biao zhang)

Stand in riding-horse stance (ma bu), with your palms on your hips. Thrust forward with both hands, fingers together and pointing forwards. Apply power to the fingertips. Practise this movement eight times.

palm push (tui zhang)

Step forward into the left bow stance (zhou gong bu), with a follow-up step. Push your palms forward, keeping your elbows and shoulders level and all four fingers together. Apply power to the centre of your palms. Practise the movement eight times on each side.

palm hack (pi zhang)

Stand in right empty-step stance (you xu bu), with your left arm outstretched, palm facing inward. Keeping your fingers together, chop your palm downward. Apply power to the outer edge of your palm. Practise the movement eight times on each side.

elbow strikes (zhou fa)

upward elbow strike (dan zhou)

Stand in riding-horse stance (ma bu), with your fists resting on your hips. Draw both elbows upwards in a quick, forceful movement. Originate the power from your waist. Apply power to your elbows. Practise the movement eight times.

elbow press (ya yhou)

This is the single butterfly stance (dan die bu). Bend your arm across the front of your body, with your forearm to the front. Press down with your elbow. Apply power to your elbow. Practise the movement eight times on each side.

southern bridge techniques (qiao fa)

The specialist technique of southern fist is the training of the forearm in order to create powerful bridge (arm) movements.

intercept bridge (jie qiao)

Step forward into the left bow stance (zhou gong bu), with your right arm making a blocking movement to the side of your body. Rotate your forearm. Apply power to your forearm. Practise the movement eight times on each side.

chop bridge (pi qiao)

In riding-horse stance (ma bu), bring your right arm across your body. Moving from left to right, make a sideways strike at shoulder level. Apply power to the back of your forearm. Practise the movement eight times on each side.

kicking techniques

front kick (teng kong fei jiao)

1 Take two steps forward, using your left leg as a springboard.

2 Jump up and raise your right leg.

3 Snap the kick forward. Apply power to your righthand toes.

nail kick (hung ding tui)

Step forward with your right leg, placing your weight on your left leg. Kick your right leg forward, across your body, with your foot positioned at an angle. Apply power to your toes.

Practise the movement eight times on each side.

hand- and footwork in internal styles

The internal styles have many striking techniques using the fist, the palm and the hook. Here is a brief explanation of what makes each system unique.

Taijiquan is based on the eight energies of the hand, arm and shoulder, which are peng, lui, ji, an, chai, lia, jou and kou. The five stepping principles are centre, forwards, backwards, left and right. Taijiquan is a soft, light and slow exercise that features continuous circular and fluent hand and foot movements.

Baghua zhang specialises in the different eight palm techniques and features special footwork and turning of the body. It uses changing palm techniques of pushing, holding, carrying, leading, thrusting, cutting and blocking. The practitioner walks in a circle and then crisscrosses in all directions. It features swift body movements, flexible footwork and constant changes of direction.

Xingyiquan has very special fist movements known as spiral fist (luosi). Xingyiquan always starts with a stance in which the body weight is mostly on the back leg (san ti shi). The five basic fist movements are: splitting fist, crushing fist, drilling fist, cannon fist and crossing fist.

a brief history of tan tui
(northern spring leg, shaolin kung fu)

The style of kung fu/wushu that I would like to introduce to you is tan tui, northern spring leg shaolin. This is an 'external' (hard) style.

The original tan tui is called longtantui (longtan foot play). According to legend, tan tui came from the Longtan Monastery in the Shandong province, hence the name of the style. It is now more commonly known as tan tui.

Tan tui has 12 routines. The 12 routines encompass the basics of northern shaolin, and many northern schools use tan tui as a fundamental part of their teaching syllabus. Tan tui is a style in its own right, and has many training practices within its art.

In 1910, the Jingwu Sports Society incorporated tan tui into its training schedule. It has ten differing schools of martial arts and uses them as basic training within its teaching of kung fu/wushu systems.

In China, tan tui is one of the exercises included on the national curriculm. It has been highlighted as a very good discipline in helping to build personal development and for strengthening the body.

The specialist technique of tan tui is the snapping of the kicking foot, and it is because of this that the discipline has the alternative name of spring leg kung fu.

The importance of practising tan tui skills is to make each movement well co-ordinated, with a smooth transition from one stance to another. The form is practised on both sides of the body.

The stances are very low, which helps to build strength and flexibility in the legs. The punching and blocking in tan tui is performed with speed, power and vigour.

There is an old Chinese saying: 'If your attacker is strong, then you must be stronger in counterattack'. The movements of tan tui are very simple, but with the correct training, it can be a devastating art for self-defence.

tan tui – 1st section

1st section, prepare posture (ye bei)

1 Stand with your feet together, back straight and arms down by your sides. Hold your head erect.

2 Bring your fists up to your hips.

1st section, posture 1 – feet together, right thrust punch
(bing bu you chong quan)

Points to remember	
1	**Back straight.**
2	**Shoulders relaxed.**
3	**Focus energy to the right fist.**
4	**Focus eyes on the right fist.**

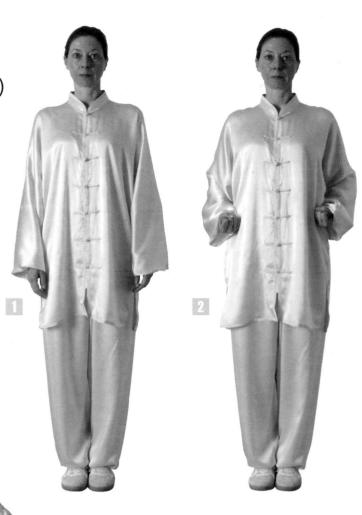

1 Keeping your feet together, bend your right elbow and then bring your fist up in front of your right shoulder.

2 Now raise your left palm above your head.

3 Turn your upper body to the right and lower your left arm, palm facing out.

4 Punch your right fist out to the right side at shoulder level. Focus your eyes on your right fist ('eye' upwards).

chapter four – KUNG FU

1st section, posture 2 – riding-horse stance & elbow parry (mabu ger zhou)

Continuing from the last movement, open your left leg and sit down in the riding-horse stance. Bring your left arm across your body and press down with your left forearm. Form a fist with your left hand, 'heart' pointing upwards.

Points to remember

1	Riding-horse stance (toes pointing forward, knees in line with toes).
2	The right fist should be level with the shoulder.
3	Keep the back straight.
4	Focus energy to the left forearm.

Keep your right fist out to the right, level with your shoulder. Focus forwards, towards your left fist.

1st section, posture 3 – left forward bow stance, thrust punch (zhou gong bu chong quan)

1 From the last movement, draw your left fist into your hip.

2 Turn your body to the left, twisting your left foot. Bend your left knee into a left forward bow stance, adjusting the back heel to a 45-degree angle, and thrust-punch with your left fist, 'eye' upwards. Keep both arms in line with your shoulders and both fists clenched. Focus on the left fist.

Points to remember

1	Forward bow stance; ensure knee and toes are in alignment.
2	Knee does not extend beyond the toe.
3	Back leg straight, toe at a 45° angle.
4	Relax shoulders.
5	Focus energy to left fist.

1st section, posture 4 – riding-horse stance & elbow strike (mabu ding zhou)

Points to remember

1	Riding-horse stance; toes pointing forwards.
2	Knees in line with toes.
3	Keep back straight and head erect.
4	Focus energy to elbow.

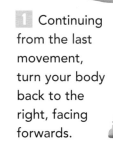

1 Continuing from the last movement, turn your body back to the right, facing forwards.

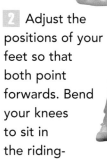

2 Adjust the positions of your feet so that both point forwards. Bend your knees to sit in the riding-horse stance.

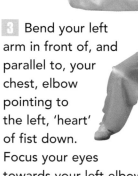

3 Bend your left arm in front of, and parallel to, your chest, elbow pointing to the left, 'heart' of fist down. Focus your eyes towards your left elbow.

1st section, posture 5 – left forward bow stance, uppercut with right fist
(zhou gong bu liao quan)

Points to remember

1	Left arm makes a blocking movement.
2	Posture alignment.
3	Right uppercut is a counterattack.
4	Focus energy on the right fist.

1 Continuing from the last movement, turn your body to the left into a left forward bow stance. Sweep your left fist down and out at knee level, and then up in line with your left shoulder, 'eye' of the fist upwards.

2 Sweep your right fist down in a forward movement.

3 Raise your arm in front of your body, chin level, 'eye' of the fist upwards. Focus your eyes on your right fist.

1st section, posture 6 – circle right fist downwards (you za quan)

1 Continuing from the last movement, circle your right fist inwards . . .

2 . . . and then downwards, using the back of the fist.

Points to remember

1	Focus energy to the back of the right fist.
2	Shoulders relaxed.
3	Focus energy to the right fist.
4	Eyes focused on the right fist.

3 Keep the right fist level with your hip and the left fist level with your left shoulder.

1st section, posture 7 – forward right snap kick (you tan tui)

This completes the first section of the routine. The next section uses the same moves, but on the other side of the body. Make sure that you are competent with the first section before moving on to the next section: it is better to learn a few movements correctly than many movements incorrectly.

1 From the last posture, keep your fists in the same position and draw your right knee up.

2 Snap your right leg forward to groin height, toes pointing forwards.

Points to remember

1	Hold your balance when you kick.
2	Back straight, head erect.
3	Focus energy to the right toe.

tan tui – 2nd section

2nd section, posture 1 – riding-horse stance, elbow parry (mabu ger zhou)

1 Continuing from the last movement, turn your body to the left and sink into riding-horse stance.

Points to remember	
1	Riding-horse stance, toes pointing forwards.
2	Knees in line with toes.
3	Keep back straight and head erect.
4	Focus energy towards the right forearm.

2 Adjust your feet so that your toes point forwards.

3 Bring your right fist in front of your body, forearm pressing down, fist's 'heart' pointing up (at chest level). Keep your left fist level with your left shoulder. Focus forwards, towards your right fist.

2nd section, posture 2 – right forward bow stance, right thrust punch (you gong bu chong quan)

1 Continuing from the last movement, draw your right fist in to your hip.

2 Turn your body to the right, turning your right foot out to the right.

3 Bend your front knee into a right forward bow stance, adjust your back heel to a 45-degree angle and thrust-punch with your right fist, 'eye' of the fist upwards. Keep both arms in line with your shoulders and your fists clenched. Focus towards your right fist.

Points to remember	
1	Forward bow stance; ensure that knee and toes are in alignment.
2	Knee should not extend beyond the toes.
3	Back leg straight, toes at a 45-degree angle.
4	Relax the shoulders.
5	Focus energy towards the right fist.

2nd section, posture 3 – riding-horse stance, elbow strike (ma bu ding zhou)

Points to remember	
1	Riding-horse stance; toes pointing forwards.
2	Knees in line with toes.
3	Keep back straight and head erect.
4	Focus energy towards the elbow.

1 Continuing from the last movement, turn your body to the left, hook your right foot around and adjust your left foot so that both feet point forward. Bend your knees and sink into riding-horse stance. Bend your right arm parallel to, and in front of, your chest.

2 Point your elbow to the right, 'heart' of the fist downwards. Keep your left fist parallel with your left shoulder. Focus towards your right elbow.

2nd section, posture 4 – right forward bow stance (you gong bu; liao quan)

1 Continuing from the last movement, turn your body to the right into a right forward bow stance. Sweep your right fist down and across at knee level, and up, in line with your right shoulder, 'eye' of your fist upwards.

2 Sweep your left fist down, in a forward movement, to uppercut in front of your body at chin level, 'eye' of your fist upwards. Focus on your left fist.

Points to remember	
1	The right arm makes a blocking movement.
2	Posture alignment.
3	The right uppercut is a counterattack.
4	Energy focus on the left fist.

2nd section, posture 5 – circle left fist downwards (zhou za quan)

2 Then circle your left fist downwards.

1 Continuing from the last movement, circle your left fist inwards.

3 Your left fist should be level with your hip, while your right fist stays level with your right shoulder. Focus on the back of your fist.

2nd section, posture 6 – left forward snap kick (zhou tan tui)

This finishes the second section of the routine. The third section is a repeat of the first section.

Practise both sections until you have committed each movement to memory.

Points to remember

1	Hold your balance when you kick.
2	Keep back straight and head erect.
3	Focus your energy on your left toes.

1 Continuing from the last movement, and keeping your fists in the same position, draw your left knee forward and up.

2 Snap your left leg forward, toes pointing forward at groin height.

closing movement (shou shi)

Practise these three sections again until you have committed the movements to memory. Train diligently.

You have now completed the first form of the northern spring leg kung fu/wushu tan tui.

Grasping the essence of tan tui will take much practice. Concentrate on building up your upper- and lower-limb co-ordination and your eye, hand and foot co-ordination to achieve the power of tan tui.

These are the basic principles of tan tui.

1 With both fists in line with your shoulders, circle your left fist over your head, changing the fist to an open hand, palm facing downwards.

2 At the same time, bring your right fist in to your hip.

3 Bring your left foot in, level with your right, and thrust-punch with your right fist at shoulder height, with your left palm facing outwards, under your arm.

4 Focus your eyes on your right fist.

tan tui for self-protection

The majority of students practise martial arts for health and fitness reasons, and this, therefore, is the focus of regular club training. Training at competition level is far more intensive than regular club training, while the focus for self-defence training is different yet again.

The postures for self-defence are not as low as those for other purposes. Low stances are ideal for conditioning the body, for building strength, suppleness and agility. There is a Chinese saying: 'If you are strong in a low posture, when you stand normally, you are much stronger'.

The self-defence techniques that follow are a sequence of defensive manoeuvres that can be used to foil various attacks, for example: a stranglehold, a punch to the face, a grab to the front of the body, a kick to the body and grabbing the wrist.

These self-defence movements should give you an idea of how the form can work.

Every teacher will use the postures and techniques in a different way, depending on the training that they have done. It is still important to train the body on both sides so that you can react to any situation that may arise, from any angle.

Remember, however, that the best form of self-defence is not to be there in the first place.

posture 1
feet together, thrust punch (bing bu chong quan)

1 You are being strangled.

2 Turn your body so that you are side-on to your attacker. This movement protects the front of your body. Swing your outside arm behind you and up.

3 Lower your raised arm, palm downwards, to deflect the grip.

4 Thrust your opposite arm over the top of your palm.

6 Carry the thrust to the attacker's chin.

postures 2 & 3

posture 2, riding-horse stance (ma bu ger zhou) linking to
posture 3, forward bow stance & thrust punch (gong bu chong quan)

1 Turn your body and step into the riding-horse stance.

2 At the same, and using the arm nearest your attacker, strike down with your forearm on to his or her elbow. This action is not a block, but a strike.

3 Turn your body into a forward bow stance and thrust-punch into your attacker's ribs.

posture 4

riding-horse stance & elbow strike (ma bu ding zhou)

Defence from an attacker making a grab at the front of your body.

1 Step sideways into a riding-horse stance and block the attacker's grab with your forearm.

2 Grip your attacker's waist and pull your opponent forwards to unbalance him or her.

3 Turn your body into a bow stance and strike with your elbow into your attacker's ribs.

posture 5

forward bow stance, uppercut with fist (gong bu liao quan)

Defence from an attacker who is kicking forwards, towards your body.

1 In a riding-horse stance, deflect the kick by sweeping the arm nearest your attacker downwards.

2 Sweep your arm up again so that it is now under your attacker's leg.

3 Step forward into the bow stance and sweep your other fist up, into your attacker's groin.

postures 6 & 7

posture 6, circle fist downwards (za quan)
posture 7, forward snap kick (tan tui)

1 As your attacker grips your wrist, move into a riding-horse stance.

2 Circle the grasped fist inwards.

3 Thrust the grasped wrist downwards to break your attacker's grip.

4 Step forward into the bow stance and snap-kick into your attacker's groin with your opposite leg.

Aim for the attacker's groin.

ju jitsu

Ju jitsu is practised throughout the world, where it is known variously as jiujitsu, jiujutsu, jujutsu and jujitsu. All names refer to the same martial art. Whatever the spelling, the meaning is the same. Ju jitsu literally means 'gentle art' ('ju' meaning 'gentle' and 'jitsu' meaning 'art'). Ju jitsu is a grouping term for various traditional Japanese martial arts.

The basics of ju jitsu include elements such as pushing, pulling, kicking, tripping and hitting with the open hand – a term that means without weapons, although the hand itself may be a fist, open or gripping. More complex techniques, such as punching, locks, holds, throws and defensive manoeuvres, are also used, although learning them requires perseverance.

The objective of ju jitsu is to neutralise an attack by any method as quickly as possible. Ju jitsu training deals with real-life situations, so although in practice there are rules and safety considerations, ju jitsu can be very brutal. If you are faced with a real life-and-death situation, your personal safety becomes the key focus. Ju jitsu teaches you how to defend yourself and, if the need arises, to counterattack. This chapter deals with various scenarios, but possible situations are limitless, so practice is necessary in order to build up a strong base knowledge to deal with the unexpected.

Although many traditionalists dismiss ju jitsu as a sport, there is a sporting aspect to modern-day ju jitsu. Those who compete do so under predetermined rules that dictate the level of contact and suitable areas that can be targeted. There are different ju jitsu organisations, and the rules vary between each one.

This chapter should offer an insight into ju jitsu. However, it should be used as a learning tool, in addition to, not instead of, instruction from a trained jujitsuka sensei (coach).

the history of ju jitsu

Ju jitsu is a group term for many fighting forms that have been taught and practised in Japan since time immemorial. It was developed from many different teachings that either originated in Japan or were brought to Japan from nearby countries, each master teaching his own learned and adapted techniques.

Establishing the exact dates and origins of martial arts is a complex task because many masters would not readily reveal their knowledge. Often, masters of martial arts passed on their wisdom, knowledge and techniques to only a privileged few. It was rare for traditional fighting techniques to be recorded. Instead, knowledge was passed on by word of mouth – and even then, there was an element of secrecy. It was common for masters to withhold key elements of their knowledge to be shared only with an approved successor. If no suitable candidate was found, the knowledge died with the master, unless the master's followers were able to rediscover the technique or techniques.

ancient history

It is impossible to pinpoint exactly when ju jitsu came into existence because it has many different origins. However, an ancient Japanese legend tells of two gods, Kajima and Kadori, who are said to have reprimanded the unruly inhabitants of an eastern province using ju jitsu.

In 2674 BC, a Chinese monk called Huang-Di founded wu-su, meaning martial arts. His concept involved the use of the body in order to defend oneself. Open-handed techniques were also reported to have been used in 772 BC in China. In 230 BC, chikura kurabe, a wrestling sport, became integrated into ju jitsu training. In AD 525, a Buddhist monk is said to have travelled from India to China, where he combined Chinese kempo (known as 'kenpo' in Japan) with yoga breathing. The monk eventually developed this technique into go-shin-jutsu-karate, meaning 'self-defence art of the open hand'.

In Japan, there is evidence of the existence of open-handed techniques during the Heian period (AD 794–1185). These techniques were used in conjunction with weapons training for the samurai warriors. In AD 880, the Daito-ryu Aiki Ju-Jitsu School was founded by Prince Teijun. This school taught secret shugendo techniques, and these eventually became the basis of kendo, using circular hand movements to combat an assailant with weapons. In 1532, Hisamori Tenenuchi formed the Tenenuchi Ryu school of ju jitsu in Japan, and he has

received much of the accreditation for founding the formal art of ju jitsu. Many fighting techniques taught at the Tenenuchi Ryu school in Japan originated from a more ancient form of combat, sumai (an ancient form of sumo). Many other similar systems, differing slightly in points of emphasis and in name, were formulated around that time. In 1559, a monk called Chin Gen Pinh migrated from China to Japan, bringing with him the art of kempo. Certain aspects of kempo became integrated into present day ju jitsu. Ju jitsu flourished throughout the Tokugawa era in Japan as it was an integral part of samurai training.

It was not until the 1900s that Japanese masters took their combative skills abroad. Then, ju jitsu was one of the first martial arts to be seen in Western society. At specially organised displays, jujitsuka demonstrated their amazing power and control, encouraging challengers, including those trained in boxing and wrestling – sometimes even two at a time! Westerners had never seen such effective and complex manoeuvres. Most challengers were reduced to submission or had to withdraw due to injury.

training basics

To achieve skills in ju jitsu, you need to practise throws and joint locks with a partner. For optimum safety, you need to learn how to fall correctly, as well as what the submission signals are and when you should give them.

dojo and tatame

Ju jitsu is practised in a dojo. A tatame (mat) is usually used for safety when training, particularly for throwing and ground work. Of course, a real-life fighting situation could occur anywhere!

The ju jitsu tatame, or mat, has to be of sufficient density to absorb the force of the body landing on it. All walls and obstacles should be covered in protective material.

judogi and zori

Ju jitsu is usually practised wearing a gi, consisting of trousers, jacket and belt. The theory behind this is that if attacked, an attacker is highly likely to be clothed. However, everyday clothes would not be able to withstand frequent training sessions.

A jujitsuka usually trains with bare feet. Traditionally, zori were worn to and from the place of practice. Zori are similar to flip-flops, but are made from straw.

The loose-fitting gi allows freedom of movement.

etiquette

Respect is a major part of ju jitsu. A jujitsuka should respect his or her sensei (coach) and other jujitsuka. The rei (bow) is an expression of respect and consideration signified by a standing bow (ritsurei) or kneeling bow (zarei). A jujitsuka performs a ritsurei when entering and leaving the dojo, and a zarei as a group to the highest grade at the beginning and end of a practice. A jujitsuka always bows to an opponent before and after a practice. The philosophy behind this is to show respect for your place of training, your sensei, your opponents and ju jitsu itself. Other factors, such as hygiene and self-discipline, are also fundamental aspects of ju jitsu.

Zarei

The starting position.

Full rei position.

The starting position for a kneeling bow.

Full kneeling bow.

Ritsurei

The starting position for a standing bow.

Front view of the standing bow.

Full standing bow.

Front view of the full standing bow.

submission

When practising elbow locks, wrist locks, knee locks and strangles, a partner can submit so as not to be injured or permanently damaged. This submission is indicated by a double tap of the hand on the tori's body (usually the arm, back or leg) or by double-tapping the ground or mat with either the hand or foot. As a last resort, a verbal submission ('Matte!', meaning 'I give up') can be used. However, in a real-life threatening situation, there is no such thing as 'I give up'!

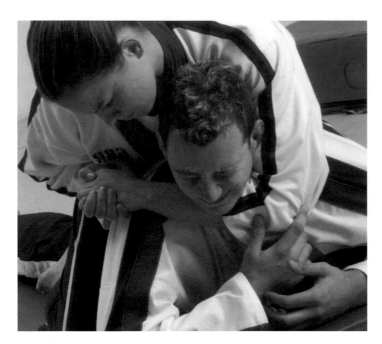

defences to attacks

All of the techniques in this chapter are demonstrated to the right; this has been done to prevent confusion. However, if you are left-handed, these techniques can be converted accordingly, i.e., substitute 'right' for 'left' in the explanations. In fact, it is useful to practise techniques on both sides as this helps to prevent any muscular imbalances and serves to confuse an assailant.

The person who is being attacked is called 'the uke'. However, when the person being attacked defends him- or herself, he or she then becomes 'the tori' (the person executing the technique). To save confusion, in this chapter, 'the tori' will always be used to indicate the jujitsuka who is responding to an attack. 'The uke' will refer to the jujitsuka who is being countered, despite his or her original attack.

The major objective of the ju jitsu throw invariably requires the uke to land flat on his or her back and, depending on the surface (i.e., concrete or hard wood), this may seriously wind or damage him or her. The

uke will certainly be in a disorientated state, even if he or she has not been seriously injured, and the tori should follow through with an atemi waza technique (straight punch or kick) while the uke is in this position. The uke can also be thrown on to the head or shoulder joint, rendering him or her unconscious or incapacitated.

terminology

'The uke' is the aggressor, on whom the counter-manoeuvre is being performed.

'The tori' is the person who is responding to the initial attack and is executing the final technique.

'Waza' means 'techniques' (i.e., atemi waza: striking techniques; nage waza: throwing techniques; tachi waza: standing techniques; and newaza: ground techniques).

ukemi waza (break-fall techniques)

Ukemi waza, or break-fall techniques, are specially designed moves used to protect the body when being thrown. These break-fall techniques are one of the major training aids for the throwing elements of ju jitsu. Ukemi waza allow throwing techniques to be practised without the risk of injury. It takes a lot of practice to allow the body to relax as you are being thrown – the initial reaction tends to be to tense up.

Break-fall techniques are usually first practised close to the ground to lessen the impact and to allow the jujitsuka to gain confidence and perfect the correct technique before advancing to an upright position. It is important to learn break falls on both sides as an opponent could be left- or right-handed, or even ambidextrous. In order to learn these techniques correctly, beginners should seek the advice and guidance of a qualified ju jitsu sensei (or else a judo sensei).

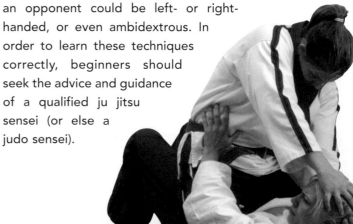

atemi waza (striking techniques)

Anyone can kick or punch; these are basic instincts used for defence. However, it is important to develop the correct kicking, punching and blocking techniques in order to minimise the risk of injury. Although these techniques use the hands to punch and the legs to kick, most techniques require rotation of the hips as this is important to increase effectiveness and force. The advice of a ju jitsu sensei should be sought in order to learn and establish good technique.

When performing the moves in atemi waza, it is essential for the tori's balance to be kept stable at all times. Strikes and blows should be aimed at the uke's vulnerable areas. However, it is important to remember that when selecting an area for attack, the idea is not to aim for the surface of the opponent's body, but to punch or kick through the target area.

tsuki waza (punching techniques)

forming a fist

Close your hand, pulling your fingers tight into your palm. The two fingers furthest from the thumb are connected to the major muscle group in the forearm, assist with the grip and also make the wrist strong. The fist should be flexed in order to get the two striking knuckles to protrude. It is important not to leave the thumb sticking out or to tuck it under the fingers as injury may occur. The thumb wraps around the index finger, pulling it in tight. The line of power should extend from the shoulder all the way through to the first two knuckles. This is achieved by ensuring that there is a straight line from the shoulder to the wrist and the top of the hand.

screw punch

The hand is clenched into a fist, knuckles facing downwards. A screw action ensues; by rotating the fist 180 degrees just prior to contact, greater force is generated. It is because of its potentially devastating effects that this type of punch is banned from boxing.

1 Stance and hand position.　　**2** Punching action.　　**3** Potential target and body position.

haishu uchi (back-hand strike)

This move is made with a partially clenched fist, with the top two joints of the thumb and fingers pulled in under the hand, keeping the rest of the hand straight.

1 Stance and hand position.　　**2** Punching action.　　**3** Potential target and position.

tettsui uchi (hammer-fist strike)

The hand is formed into a fist and the side of the hand, along the little finger, is used to strike, usually the top of the head.

head

1 Stance and hand position.   **2** Punching action.

3 Potential target and position.

straight punch

1 Stance and hand position for a side-fist punch.

2 Punching action for a straight punch.

uppercut punch

1 Stance and hand position for a knuckle-back punch.

2 Punching action for an uppercut punch.

keri waza (kicking techniques)

Kicks are usually aimed low as they are safer to execute. As a rule of thumb, the higher you kick, the less stable you become. Furthermore, a high kick can be countered by a jujitsuka, and if a leg is caught, you can be thrown to the ground. It is also important that the tori's balance is secure, which can be difficult as most kicks are performed on one leg. Successful kicking techniques rely on considerable flexibility of the groin and hip, and it is important to learn the correct techniques when kicking or punching.

mawashi geri (roundhouse kick)

The knee is raised and turned approximately 90 degrees; the leg is extended, making contact with the side of the aggressor, using either the ball or the top of the foot to perform the kick.

1 Lifting action.

2 Striking action.

3 Potential target area.

ushiro geri (rear kick)
straight

The body weight is taken on one foot, while the other leg is raised and driven straight backwards. For a more powerful and accurate kick, pivot 90 degrees before raising the other leg, then drive the foot backwards. The heel or the side of the foot is used to strike.

1 Body position and lifting action.

2 Back-kicking action.

3 Potential target area.

fumi komi (stamp kick)

This is usually used for stamping on an aggressor's toes or instep, or is applied when an assailant is on the ground (possibly following a throw).

1 Stance and start of lifting action.

2 Continuation of lifting action.

3 Kicking action.

1 Completion of flying kick.

tobe geri (flying kick)

There are various flying kicks, but although they are spectacular, they require much practice and accuracy. If they are not performed correctly, they are counterproductive.

2 Potential target area.

uki waza (blocking techniques)

Usually, the forearms are used to deflect kicks and blows. By clenching the fists, the muscles are tensed in the forearms. The forearm is used to block most hand attacks by rotating it upwards, and low hand attacks and kicks by rotating it downwards.

A jujitsuka encounters many situations and has to adapt to them. Blocking techniques are important because they serve to protect the body. There are many ways of blocking as there are many situations that may arise. Once the basic principles of blocking have been established, a jujitsuka can make subtle changes to adapt these blocks to the situation at hand. These techniques should be practised on the left, as well as the right. To build up a good technique and to prevent injury, always practise unfamiliar movements slowly and gradually increase the speed. With practice, confidence is built. Once a jujitsuka is proficient in these blocks, they can be used in combination with, and in addition to, striking and throwing techniques.

nagashi uke (sweeping block)

This is probably the most frequently used block to a kick attack. The tori's stance should be legs apart, one foot slightly in front of the other (in this instance, right foot in front of the left), with the knees slightly bent. The tori, keeping an open hand, rotates the hand and arm in an anti-clockwise direction and uses the palm to cup and/or push the uke's attacking arm or leg away. Alternatively, the tori can keep hold of it and follow up with a throwing or striking technique of his or her own. The tori must use the palm of the hand for this technique as the fingers can become injured.

1 Start position.

2 Blocking action.

3 The full blocking action.

4 Leg-grabbing action following the block.

age uke (raising block)

This is a powerful block. It is used to prevent attacks to the chest, face and head region of the body. It requires precision and speed, and therefore practice, to be effective. The tori has her right foot in front of her left, with the knees slightly bent. The tori clenches her right fist and drives it across her body, pushing it up and forwards simultaneously. The thrusting action should be derived from the hip. The tori rotates her right arm so that the back of it is facing her.

1 Starting position.

2 Hand and arm movement.

3 Blocking action.

soto ude uke (outside forearm block)

This technique deflects attacks aimed at the centre of the body. The tori has her right foot in front of the left, knees slightly bent. The tori clenches her fists, with her right arm bent at the elbow. The right elbow is lowered, pushing the arm across the tori's body to the left, and rotated in a clockwise direction, turning the hand so that the knuckles are foremost.

1 Starting position.

2 Movement of the body.

3 Blocking action.

juji barai (cross-block)

This blocking action is normally used for defence against a straight kick. Crossing the arms and making a fist strengthens a blocking action. Once the block is successful, the tori can grab the uke's leg and counter with a kick. Alternatively, the tori can push the uke's leg to one side and perform a throw.

1 Starting position.

2 Arm and fist block.

3 Full blocking action.

triangular grip break

The triangular grip break is a method used to break an aggressor's double lapel grip or front strangle. The fists, palms or entangled fingers are placed together between the aggressor's arms and the arms are driven upwards to break the grip, following which various options are open for the tori to attack.

1 Stance and hand position.

2 Breaking the grip.

osaekomi waza (immobilisation)

The objective is to immobilise or hold and control the body with a joint lock, which limits the uke's movement or chance of escape. Joint locks are used to achieve a holding action or to force a submission in training. It is also possible to incapacitate an assailant with joint dislocations.

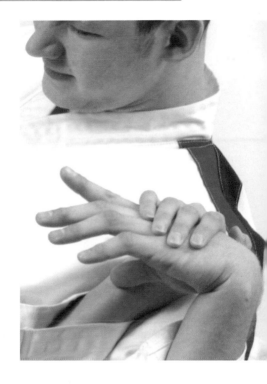

Major joints that can be attacked to achieve immobilisation are the wrists and elbows (which tend to be somewhat stronger than the wrists). Knees and ankle joints are also vulnerable, as are the neck and spine. The level of force and speed applied will determine the amount of damage that can be inflicted. A ju jitsu move that is made too fast can result in permanent damage to a joint. In the case of the neck or spine, an incorrect holding action could be fatal.

kote waza (wrist locks)

These grips are used to apply wrist locks. The wrist tends to be the weakest of all of the joints when it comes to immobilisation. Once a grip is established, the wrist joint is attacked by rotating the hand against its natural range of movement. This creates pain and the uke loses balance through endeavouring to reposition his or her body in a bid to stop the pain. A firm grip is essential for success.

back of the hand, thumb-to-thumb grasp

The tori grips the uke's hand by placing her right thumb on the base of the uke's thumb. The tori's fingers grip tightly around the rest of the hand to the little-finger side of the hand. The tori twists the uke's hand in a clockwise direction, pushing the hand towards the forearm. Pressure is exerted on the wrist joint. If the tori continues the twisting action, the uke is forced face down to the ground. Pressure is now applied to the wrist using a twisting motion, while pushing the uke's palm towards her forearm.

1 Hand position.   **2** Direction of technique.

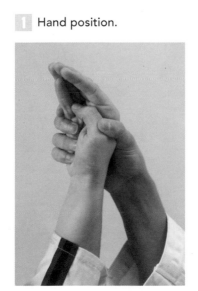

wrist lock from a wrist grab

The uke grabs the tori's wrist with her right hand, fingers over the wrist. The tori executes a knife action with her hand and rotates her wrist, aiming for the uke's little finger to touch the uke's wrist. The tori continues rotating her own wrist after gripping the uke's wrist, with her other hand placed on the uke's elbow joint. The uke is taken down to the ground with a half-circle action.

1 The uke's attacking grip.

2 Start of the wrist action.

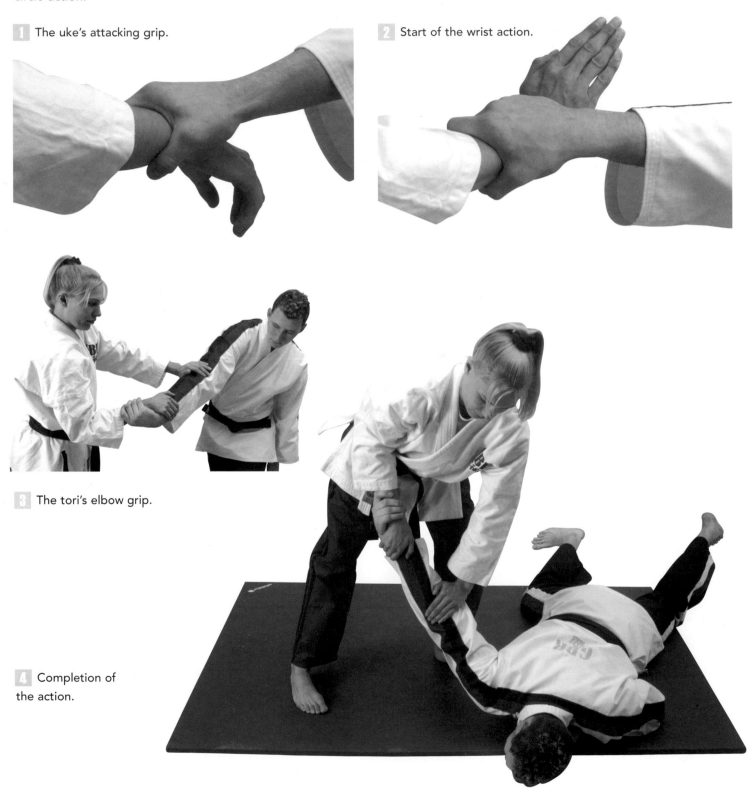

3 The tori's elbow grip.

4 Completion of the action.

kansetsu waza (arm locks)

An effective arm lock is applied to the elbow in these techniques. The moves also rely on a wrist lock, from which more pressure is applied. The tori uses various parts of his or her body as a lever base.

ude gatame (straight arm lock)

The tori grasps the uke's arm at the wrist and turns the arm so that the wrist is pointing upwards. The tori takes her other hand over the uke's arm and under the uke's elbow, placing her hand on top of the uke's forearm to create a pivot to apply pressure. This can be done while on the inside or outside of the uke's arms.

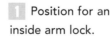 **1** Position for an inside arm lock.

2 Position for an outside arm lock.

eri gatame (collar hold)

From a standing position to the uke's right side, the tori grabs the uke's right wrist. The tori's fingers clasp the inner wrist and twist the arm in an anti-clockwise direction. At the same time, the tori places her left arm under the uke's armpit and grabs the opposite collar, with the fingers inside the jacket. Pressure is put on the uke's elbow joint with a twisting action applied to the uke's right arm.

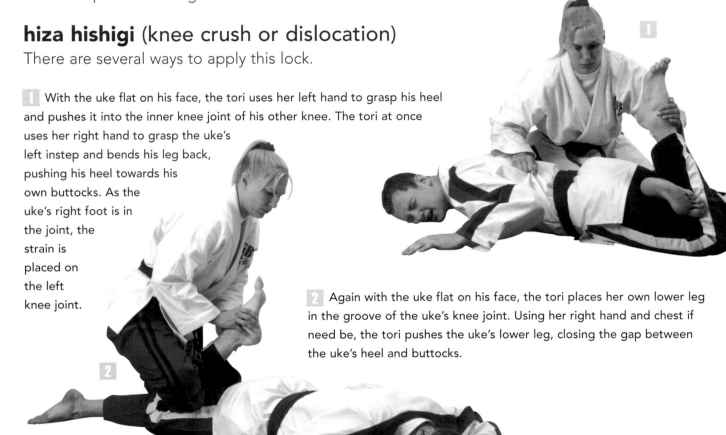

ashi kansetsu waza (leg locks)

The objective of leg locks is, in the first instance, to apply pressure against the weakest joint, which tends to be the knee. As with locks to any other joint, precise positioning is necessary in order to apply a technique successfully. Not all leg locks apply pressure to the knee or ankle joints: some cause immense pain to the leg muscles.

hiza hishigi (knee crush or dislocation)

There are several ways to apply this lock.

1 With the uke flat on his face, the tori uses her left hand to grasp his heel and pushes it into the inner knee joint of his other knee. The tori at once uses her right hand to grasp the uke's left instep and bends his leg back, pushing his heel towards his own buttocks. As the uke's right foot is in the joint, the strain is placed on the left knee joint.

2 Again with the uke flat on his face, the tori places her own lower leg in the groove of the uke's knee joint. Using her right hand and chest if need be, the tori pushes the uke's lower leg, closing the gap between the uke's heel and buttocks.

ashi kannuki (leg bolt lock)

The tori is lying on her back, with the uke transversally on top (chest to chest). The tori traps the uke's right leg by entangling her right leg around his leg and hooking his instep under her own left lower leg. The tori then pushes the toes of the left foot up, trapping the top of his foot. The tori pulls his body in tight and straightens her legs to apply the lock.

kata ashi hishigi (single-leg crush or dislocation)

This technique can be applied from three different positions, but the result is the same.

1 With the tori standing. When the uke is on his back, the tori stands in front, by his feet. The technique is easier if the tori is slightly to one side, so she steps to her left and traps the uke's right ankle under her armpit, squeezing tight and securing the position by taking her right arm under the uke's leg and clenching her other hand for support. The tori bends back while maintaining a strong grip of the uke's leg and pressing her forearm into his lower-leg or calf region, using her body weight to apply pressure to the ankle joint. The effectiveness of the lock can be increased by pushing sideways.

2 With the tori in a seated position. This technique can be applied with the same grip of the uke's leg under the tori's armpit, but this time the tori is seated, supporting herself with her right leg. Her left leg is stretched diagonally across the uke's abdomen. The tori then leans backwards. Alternatively, to apply the lock to the knee joint, she squeezes her knees to clamp the uke's leg tightly, and instead of leaning straight back, she leans to the left and pushes inwards, with her left knee pressing on the uke's outer knee.

3 With the uke flat on his front and the tori standing. Another single-leg lock can be applied either when the uke is lying flat on his stomach or as a continuation of the first version, described above, when the uke is struggling. While maintaining the grip on the uke's leg, the tori steps with her left leg over the uke's held leg. The uke has no choice but to turn onto his front. The tori bends her knees to give herself a solid base and then leans back, applying pressure to the uke's leg.

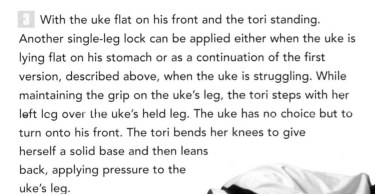

kubi kansetsu waza (spine locks)

These techniques are potentially the most dangerous in ju jitsu, the aim being to twist the neck where it meets the spine. The moves can be used to immobilise an opponent when fighting on the ground, and can be fatal if applied incorrectly.

kubi hishigi
(dislocation neck lock/neck crush)

The uke is on her back and the tori sits astride the uke, with one or both knees on the ground. The tori sits on the uke's chest, towards her head. The tori places one hand over the other on the back of the uke's head and pulls the uke's head forwards. Increased pressure is added by taking the head to one side while maintaining the forward pressure.

oase hishigi
(dislocation in immobilisation)

The uke is on her back and the tori sits astride the uke, with either one or both knees on the ground. The tori supports himself with his left arm and leans forwards, moving his head towards the uke's right shoulder. The tori then slides his right arm under the uke's neck and bends his arm backwards to grip his own belt (so that the back of the tori's hand makes contact with his own hip area as he grasps the belt). The uke's head is clamped under the tori's armpit as the tori pushes against the mat with his left hand and bends to his back-righthand corner.

defence against attacks – possible responses

tai otoshi (body drop)

The tori requires an upright posture in a preparation stance, one leg slightly forward. As the uke swings the punch, the tori blocks. The blocking arm immediately bends at the wrist, takes the uke's forearm (or cloth in that region, if available) and pulls with a semi-circular action. At the same time, the tori swings her left leg back, which rotates her body and shoulders. The tori places her other arm around the uke's head and rotates the uke's body over her right leg, which is blocking the uke's right leg. This action uses the uke's momentum from the throwing of the punch. If the tori maintains her grip on the uke's arm, she can pull down so that the uke ends up on his face and an ude gatame (an arm lock) is applied.

1 Starting position.

2 Blocking action.

3 Gripping action.

4 Rotation entry.

5 Throwing position.

6 Direction of throw.

ago tsuki (uppercut)

The tori blocks the uke's punch and swings into an uppercut. When executing the uppercut, the wrist is launched from the waist level. The tori can target the point on the chin if the uke's stance is upright, but quite often the mechanics of the thrown punch have the uke leaning forwards, so that the target of the punch is then the throat.

1 Starting position.

2 Blocking position.

3 Target position of the punch.

avoidance using an outside block

The following techniques use a different principle, avoidance of the initial attack, rather than just blocking and attacking. The tori steps back and applies forearm blocks to the outside of the thrown punch. This action tends to overextend the uke's punching arm rather than block it.

osoto gari
(major outer sweep)

Avoidance block. The uke steps forwards with his right leg as the right arm slides from the block across the uke's face and the hand is placed on the shoulder. The tori steps behind and leans forwards, simultaneously pulling the uke's head back. She then sweeps with her leg.

1 Starting position.

1 Blocking action.

3 Start of stepping action.

4 Continuation of stepping action.

5 Sweeping action.

complete MARTIAL ARTS guide

gyaku ogoshi (reverse major hip throw)

The tori avoids the punch and blocks to the outside. The tori's arm goes around the uke's head and the tori steps behind the uke, placing the rear of her hip into the uke's back and throwing him over her hips.

1 Starting position.

2 Blocking action.

3 Start of stepping action.

4 Placement of hip.

5 Lifting action.

6 Full throwing action.

182

ude gatame (arm lock)

The tori avoids the attack with a block. The blocking arm slides down the uke's arm until the tori can grasp his wrist. The tori's other arm transfers over and the palm is placed on the uke's elbow. Simultaneously, the tori pulls the uke's arm with the wrist grip and circles with her arm and his body, gradually getting the arm lower to the ground until the uke is flat on his face. The tori could stay in position and immobilise, or kneel on the arm and pull back the wrist and the arm will then break.

1 Starting position.

2 Blocking position.

3 Start of hand control.

4 Continuation of hand control.

5 The tori's body position.

6 The tori's body position.

7 Continuation of arm control.

8 Completion of technique.

punch to the stomach

The uke aims a punch at the tori's solar-plexus muscle group. This punch is launched in a screwing action from the uke's waist level. The tori's initial response is to block the punch.

sumi otoshi (floating drop)

The tori blocks the front punch with a gedan barai (downward block), and at same time steps towards the uke's side. The tori's other hand is placed at the side of the uke's head. The tori's blocking arm wraps down and around the uke's punching arm and pushes the head sideways as hard as possible. This pins the uke's weight on to his right foot and throws him to the ground. This is a complete hand throw: none of the tori's other body parts make contact.

1 Starting position.

2 Blocking action.

3 Stepping action.

4 Throwing action.

184

atama waza (head butt)

The tori blocks the punch, parrying the hand outwards. The tori then closes down the space and uses her forehead to strike the front of the uke's face, either directly on the nose or above it (the bridge). The tori can make the attack stronger by simultaneously grasping the back of the uke's head (his neck) and pulling her head forwards. The tori must be accurate when using her forehead, otherwise she could herself be knocked out!

1 Starting position.

2 Blocking action.

3 Gripping action.

4 Head action.

5 Completion of technique.

attack with single-lapel grab

An initial grab attack starts with one hand first. The object of the series of responses is to attack before the other hand also grabs or a possible blow is attempted. The surprise element is very much a part of the response to the initial one-hand lapel grab.

kani basami (leg scissors)

The tori grips the uke's left lapel with her right hand. The tori jumps into position, placing her right leg across the front of the uke's thighs and her left leg behind the knees or calf region. The tori then pushes back with her right leg and forwards with her left, hence the 'basami', or 'scissors', part of the name. The uke falls to his rear.

1 The tori attacking – lapel grab. 2 Continuation of leg attack. 3 Completion of the technique.

kani garami (crab entanglement)

The tori attempts kani basami, but the uke resists by leaning forwards. In response, the tori changes the direction of rotation (rolling in a clockwise direction). The front of the tori's left leg pushes the uke's ankles or shins and the back of the tori's right leg pushes the uke's knees at the back. In this instance, the uke falls on to his front.

1 Initial cross-lapel grab. 2 First leg attacking position. 3 Second leg attacking position. 4 Completion of throw.

attack with double-lapel grip

From in front of the tori, the uke grips the lapels or cloth with both hands. This is a common initial attack from the uke, which is initially used to control the tori. It can then develop into a head butt or push. If the attacker is very skilled, there are many throws that can be attempted from this grip.

hiza strike (knee strike)

The tori brings a knee sharply up into the uke's groin. If the uke's stance is a bit to one side, the knee strike could be to the front of the thigh, which can numb the leg.

3 Completion of the action.

1 The uke's double-lapel grip.

2 The tori's initial gripping response.

the triangular grip break

The triangular grip break consists of breaking the double-lapel grip by placing the fists or palms together or using an entangled-finger grip and driving the arms upwards. The following techniques can be used following this break.

sasae tsurikomi ashi (propping drawing ankle)

Using a triangular grip break, the tori immediately wraps the uke's right arm with her left arm, simultaneously stepping to the side and blocking the front of the uke's foot as he steps forwards. The tori's other arm comes up under the uke's armpit. The pulling action is over the tori's left shoulder. To make the fall extremely heavy, the tori falls on top of the uke's chest (ribcage).

1 Uke's double-lapel grip.

2 Breaking uke's grip.

3 Tori's grip on uke's arm.

4 Stepping into body contact.

5 Completion of throw.

grab from behind

A major attacking move can be made from behind. When the uke attacks the tori in this way by surprise, the objective is to immobilise the tori's arms or body. The head is controlled by a neck hold or attempted strangle. The tori can respond with either throws or strikes.

ashi dori (leg grab)

The tori leans forwards and grips one of the uke's legs, pulling the leg through her own legs and falling backwards, aiming to sit on the uke's stomach. This will wind the uke.

1 Double-outside-arm attack.

2 Start of body action.

3 Hand placement.

4 Lifting action.

5 Completion of throw.

grab around the waist

The uke grabs the tori around the waist from behind. As with the grab around the arms, the tori has her back to the uke. The grip occurs when the tori's arms are not close to her body.

harai makikomi (winding sweeping hip)

The tori reaches across and takes the uke's wrist, simultaneously moving her leg to the outside of the uke's right leg. The tori leans forwards and starts to rotate, which brings the uke up onto his toes. The tori then makes a sweeping action with her outside leg.

1 Double-outside-arm waist attack.

2 Tori's hand and arm position.

3 Tori's hand and leg position.

4 Completion of throw.

grab around the neck

The uke grabs the tori around the neck from behind, a common attack when an opppent's back is to the uke. Depending on the uke's aims, the move can control the tori, render her unconscious or kill her.

sukui nage (scoop throw)

The tori leans forwards while simultaneously stepping sideways. Placing her left leg behind the uke, the tori reaches down and takes both of his legs, lifting straight back and falling on the uke.

1 Attacking position.

2 The tori's hand position.

3 Body positioning.

4 Leg grab.

5 Throwing action.

defence against kicks – possible responses

Predominantly, there are three methods of kicking. There is a front kick, which normally uses the top of the foot or the toes and involves taking the leg straight up into the uke's body. Then there is the roundhouse kick, which involves swinging the leg and foot in a semi-circular motion. Lastly, there is the straight kick, which is delivered by the side of the foot, normally to the lower half of the uke's body. Most kicks that are effective do not travel above waist height. It is possible to deliver kicks to the chest, neck and face, but inevitably power is lost and the tori's balance is compromised.

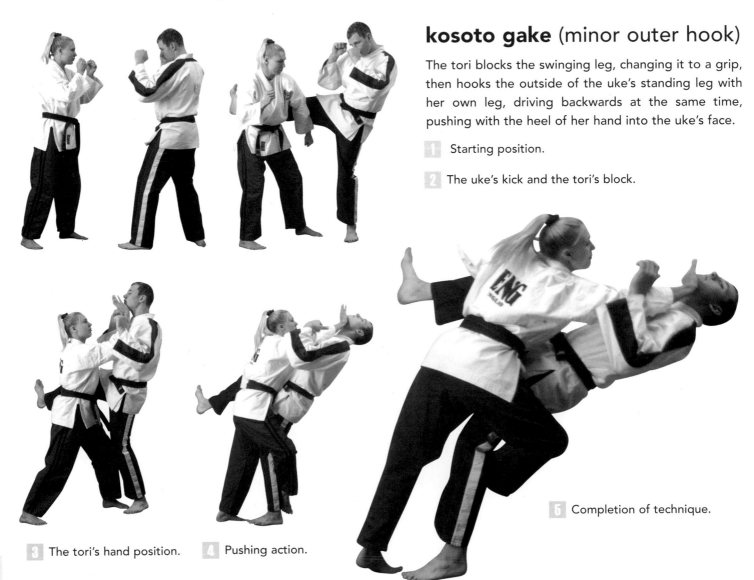

kosoto gake (minor outer hook)

The tori blocks the swinging leg, changing it to a grip, then hooks the outside of the uke's standing leg with her own leg, driving backwards at the same time, pushing with the heel of her hand into the uke's face.

1 Starting position.

2 The uke's kick and the tori's block.

3 The tori's hand position.

4 Pushing action.

6 Completion of technique.

ankle twist

After the initial movement is blocked, the tori grasps the uke's ankle and the toes of the striking leg and twists.

1 Starting position.

2 The uke's kick and the tori's block.

3 Gripping action.

4 Twisting action.

5 Completion of technique.

newaza (ground techniques)

In a fight, it is quite usual to end up on the ground. In a one-on-one situation, there are many techniques that can be used. The positions are normally either the tori on her back with the uke on top, or the uke on his back with the tori on top. With ju jitsu techniques, there is a wide range of moves that can be used when the tori is supine (on her back).

The ground-fighting techniques shown here involve strangles, neck locks and leg locks. The objectives and skills of ground-work fighting involve being able to control an opponent before he or she attempts any of these techniques. Control is normally gained by using the legs and body weight, together with the positioning of the hands. Strangles are used because the neck area is very vulnerable in ground-fighting situations. The main principle used is the exertion of pressure on the carotid artery, situated on either side of the neck. The artery is protected by the neck muscles, but the action of a grip tends to move the muscles to one side.

tori in a supine position (hold-downs)

All of the techniques shown are attempted when the tori immediately positions herself in a defensive grappling position on her back and gets the uke between her legs.

These strangles can also be executed when the tori is on top of the uke, sitting astride his stomach. Quite often, the strangle will be initiated while the tori is underneath, and she will use her legs to turn the uke over.

shimi waza (strangles)

The objective of these strangle techniques is to exert pressure on the carotid artery, which is located in the neck below the earlobes, following the line of the jaw. It is assumed that the opponent or aggressor will be wearing normal clothing – a shirt with a collar or a coat, represented by a gi.

gyaku juji jime (reverse cross-strangle)

The uke is between the tori's legs and is being controlled by the tori with a do jime technique. Do jime is a squeezing scissor action of the legs. The tori reaches across with her right hand to the uke's collar, with her fingers inside the collar, and does the same to the other lapel with the other hand. The grip needs to be deep enough to place the cutting edge of the inside of the arm level with the carotid artery. The tori then pulls the uke's head towards her. This creates a scissor action against the carotid artery, and if positioned correctly, the uke will, for training purposes, submit or in a real life threatening situation, become unconscious.

ryote jime (double-handed strangle)

The tori grasps the outside of the uke's collar on either side of the neck, positioning the knuckles level with the carotid artery. The tori then rotates her fists inwards, towards the carotid artery. She then lifts her legs to the uke's shoulders, crossing her legs and applying pressure with her fists.

tsuri komi jime (thrusting strangle)

The tori grasps the far lapel of the uke's jacket, thumb inside, and grips the opposite lapel, fingers inside and the hand turned so that the thumb is pointing down. The tori then pushes the lapel under the uke's chin and drives into the throat area. The knuckle grip is level with the carotid artery to apply the strangle.

sode guruma jime (sleeve wheel strangle)

The tori throws her forearm across the back of the uke's neck and the other forearm goes under the uke's throat. The tori's hands then grasp her own sleeves; quite often, this is a choke on the windpipe rather than being applied to the carotid artery.

uke in a defensive posture

The uke is lying flat, face down in a defensive posture. This position is normally adopted by the uke after having been thrown to the ground. The position is purely defensive. The tori can make a number of moves to control the uke.

hadaku jime (naked strangle)

The tori jumps on the uke's back and maintains control by hooking her legs under his thighs. The tori then places her chest on the uke's back and pushes her body into the ground, simultaneously lifting her hooked-in legs onto the uke's thighs. This action exerts pressure on the spinal area. Simultaneously, the tori slides a straight hand under the uke's chin and grabs her other hand. The tori applies pressure to the back of the neck by pulling back, using her own chest as a block.

kata ha jime (single-collar strangle)

The tori jumps on the uke's back, hooks her legs in and pushes her hips into the small of his back. The tori slides her hand under the uke's chin and grasps, thumb inside, fingers outside, endeavouring to get her wrist action level with the furthest carotid-artery region of the neck. The tori's other hand comes under his armpit and, with the palm down on the back of his neck, the tori pushes his head forward and rotates using a semi-circular action to apply the strangle.

chapter six

kickboxing

Kickboxing is a relatively modern martial art that combines boxing techniques with kicks. A combat sport, kickboxing has its roots in traditional martial arts, including as it does techniques from karate, Thai boxing, tae kwon do and kung fu.

Martial arts gained in popularity during the early 1970s, and karate practitioners in America soon became frustrated with the strict controls and rules entrenched in set rituals that did not allow full-contact kicks and punches and fights to the knockout. They wanted to see how effective their fighting style was in a realistic situation.

And so it was that kickboxing originated in the United States, where traditional martial arts took on a more Westernised style, and where those of their practitioners who wanted to concentrate on tournament fighting were inspired to develop kickboxing.

Kickboxing is different from traditional combat sports like Thai boxing in that it prohibits strikes with the elbows and knees. All of the techniques practised in this combat sport are directed above the belt.

Because of the great emphasis that was placed on specialised punching and kicking techniques being used at maximum force against an opponent, questions were raised about safety and the high risk of injury in this new sport. As a result, protective clothing like groin guards, gum shields and hand and foot pads designed to lessen the impact of the kicks and punches, as well as improved safety rules, were introduced. The most notable was the introduction of weight divisions ranging from flyweight to super heavyweight.

Such martial artists as Bill 'Superfoot' Wallis, Demetrius Havanas, Jeff Smith, Mike Warren, Joe Lewis, Blinky and his brother, Benny, were among the first generation of kickboxers involved in staging very successful events. All of these fighters were the best of the best in this new martial art. The first full-contact world championships were held in Los Angeles in September 1974, the legendary Bill Wallis, Joe Lewis, Jeff Smith and Isuena Duenas becoming the first full-contact world champions.

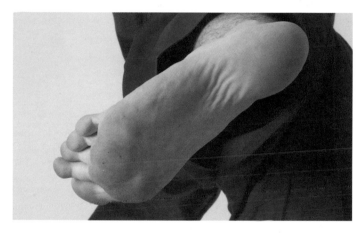

It was martial artists like Howard Hansen (a black belt in karate who was one of the main promoters of kickboxing) who first staged fights in a boxing ring instead of the usual karate tournament bouts. Hansen later became known as 'The Ring Matchmaker'.

It was in those early days that the World Kickboxing Association (WKA) was founded. The WKA became successful by finding common ground between Western and Eastern full-contact fighting culture, thereby creating and defining a culture for the sport that improved the recognition of full-contact competitions.

Today, kickboxing is a sport that is practised not just by hard-core, full-contact fighters, but also by people who want to develop strength, flexibility, stamina, fitness and well-being. These aspects of kickboxing appeal to both men and woman, whatever their background. It is not a brutal sport in which people meet in back yards and beat the hell out of each other. It is a powerful and skilful sport that improves mental agility and fitness and also promotes comradeship. Kickboxing is practised by celebrities, too, including film stars like Jean Claude van Damme, a Belgian actor whose nickname is 'The Muscles From Brussels'.

kickboxing styles

There are a lot of different styles of kickboxing. Every style has its own rules, which can differ from organisation to organisation.

Fights are normally supervised by a body affiliated to a particular organisation. The length of a fight can range from three to twelve rounds, each round being two minutes long. The rest time between the rounds is usually one minute. After each round, points are awarded. Once the final bell has been rung, the fighter with the most points is declared the winner, which is known as winning by decision. The fight can also be won by a knockout blow if a full-contact style is being fought.

Because of the nature of the sport, kicks have to be used in a fight. The general rule is that you have to place at least eight kicks per round. The points system used during fights is normally as follows: a punch =1 point; a kick to the head = 2 points; a kick to the body = 1 point; a jumping kick to the body = 2 points; a jumping kick to the head = 3 points.

In kickboxing, fights are usually divided into weight divisions. Refer to the table at right showing the different weight divisions that are specified by the World Kickboxing Association.

semi-contact

In semi-contact kickboxing, points are awarded for punches and kicks that are delivered with reasonable force. After every successful strike, the fight is stopped and points are awarded. The length of the fight is normally two rounds, each round lasting two minutes. The compulsory safety equipment is kick boots, gloves, a groin guard, a mouth guard, a shin guard and a head guard.

light contact

Light contact is an intermediate stage between the semi-contact and full-contact styles. Light contact uses controlled techniques. The fight is continuous and is not stopped after every strike as it is with semi-contact. The only time that the fight is stopped is when clinching occurs. The length of the fight is normally two rounds, each lasting two minutes, with a one-minute rest between rounds. The compulsory safety equipment is kick boots, gloves, a mouth guard, a groin guard, a shin guard and a head guard.

weight divisions: men	
Flyweight	Up to 50.5kg (111lb).
Super flyweight	Over 50.5 and up to 52kg (115lb).
Bantamweight	Over 52 and up to 53.5kg (118lb).
Super bantamweight	Over 53.5 and up to 55.5kg (122lb).
Featherweight	Over 55.5 and up to 57kg (126lb).
Super featherweight	Over 57 and up to 59kg (130lb).
Lightweight	Over 59 and up to 61kg (134lb).
Super lightweight	Over 61 and up to 63.5kg (140lb).
Welterweight	Over 63.5 and up to 67kg (148lb).
Super welterweight	Over 67 and up to 70kg (154lb).
Middleweight	Over 70 and up to 72.5kg (160lb).
Super middleweight	Over 72.5 and up to 76kg (168lb).
Light heavyweight	Over 76 and up to 79kg (174lb).
Super light heavyweight	Over 79 and up to 83kg (183lb).
Cruiserweight	Over 83 and up to 86kg (190lb).
Super cruiserweight	Over 86 and up to 90kg (198lb).
Heavyweight	Over 90 and up to 95kg (209lb).
Super heavyweight	Over 95kg (209lb).

weight divisions: women	
Women's weight divisions range from 48kg (106lb) to over 64kg (141lb), with the weight class changing every 2kg (4lb).	

full contact

Full-contact kickboxing bouts are fought in a ring. As the name suggests, full-contact fighters are allowed to throw kicks and punches at maximum power. Knockouts can therefore be seen in full-contact fights. Amateur bouts consist of three rounds, with one-minute breaks between rounds, each round lasting two minutes. The length of each fight can vary, however. Professional bouts can last for twelve rounds. The compulsory safety equipment is kick boots, gloves, a groin guard, a mouth guard, a shin guard and a head guard (but those in professional bouts will not wear head guards).

Thai boxing

Thai boxing is a full-contact sport. It is different from full-contact kickboxing, however, in that low kicks and knee and elbow strikes can be directed to the body and head. (But note that although elbow strikes are allowed in professional bouts, they are not permitted in amateur bouts.) Amateur bouts last for three rounds, with each round lasting three minutes. Professional bouts last for five rounds, with each round lasting for three minutes. The compulsory safety equipment is gloves and a gum shield. No protective gear may be worn on the legs and feet. Amateur fighters will also wear head guards, whereas professionals will not.

is kickboxing for me?

Due to modern training techniques, kickboxing has become the ultimate workout. It produces kickboxers who are strong, fast, fit and very conditioned. Kickboxing training gets you into top physical shape, toning your body by reducing body fat.

Kickboxing offers an intense cardiovascular workout. That it also teaches the art of self-defence is very appealing to a lot of people. It is therefore not surprising that taking kickboxing classes has become one of the biggest trends in the fitness industry since aerobics.

women in kickboxing

Kickboxing appeals to the young and old, to men and woman. Indeed, it is becoming increasingly popular with women as a practical means of learning to defend themselves while also becoming fit; it promotes a positive mental attitude, too. Women find the training aspects of kickboxing attractive because they can help to burn fat and quickly tone and firm the body. A lot of women today now compete internationally at the highest levels of kickboxing.

Kickboxing is additionally a practical martial art that does not seem as monotonous as many traditional martial arts. The basics can be learned in about six months.

age in kickboxing

Age does not matter in kickboxing. What does matter is that practitioners know what they want from the training. Children can start as early as ten, and it is important that parents chose a good club in which all beginner's classes are strictly no contact, progressing to controlled sparring with no contact to the head. Sparring must be closely supervised, and fully protective clothing and a head guard must be worn.

The upper age limit is a question of mental attitude. There are martial-arts' practitioners in their sixties performing workouts that some twenty-year-olds would find hard to follow. Martial arts prompt a positive mental attitude that makes barriers vanish. Remember that we set our own barriers, and that age should not be one of them.

is kickboxing a dangerous sport?

Some people think of kickboxing as being an extreme sport that is rife with injuries. This perception could not be further from the truth, and some kickboxers would assert that playing football or rugby can be a lot more injurious than kickboxing. It is important to understand that in the advanced stages, both training and sparring are closely supervised and that they consist of more than just lashing out at each other.

Communication is another important factor in training safely. Talk to your training partner to make it clear to what level you want to take it. Tell your partner either that you

want to take it easy or that you want to spar seriously.

When competition fights are fought, the fight is monitored so closely that hardly any major injuries occur.

how long does it take to learn?

The basics of kickboxing can be learned in approximately six months or so, during which time you can participate in all of the normal training routines. Mastering kicks and punches and using them in fighting strategies against different opponents can take years, however.

Sometimes, the less you think about performing techniques, the more naturally they come. This will occur the more experience you gain in kickboxing. Good kickboxers always look loose and not tense, which is one of the reasons why their reactions are faster and they do not use up as much energy as beginners.

So to answer the original question: it takes years to become a technically competent kickboxer.

do you have to be fit to practise?

As is the case with any sport, it helps to be fit to practise kickboxing, but if you are not, you should still be fine as long as you are physically healthy and don't have any serious health problems. A good club should point out that you can only do your best, and that the only person who can really push you is you yourself.

After just three months of training twice a week, you will notice the difference: you will feel fitter and will be starting to look leaner. The time when fitness is paramount is when you wish to compete because the fitter you are, the easier you will find it to survive the rounds. If you are not fit and are struggling to keep going, this is when your techniques will become slack and less powerful. To achieve fighting fitness, it is probably fair to say that you should train at least five times a week.

where do I find a good club?

The best place in which to look for a good kickboxing club is your local library, which should have an index of clubs in your area. Visit your local clubs to get a feel for them. When selecting a club, it is vital to ask yourself whether you could see yourself working with the people that train there because they will get the best out of you. A good club should have a friendly atmosphere, take pride in its safety measures and emphasise good techniques. Remember that a club should serve to teach you how to become a better fighter, not to inflict injuries on you.

what equipment do I need?

It is important to remember that you should always train with high-quality equipment, and that the equipment that you hit, or hit with, is durable.

clothing

Kickboxing trousers usually have an 8cm (3in) boxer-style, elasticated waistband. They are also generously cut to enable a lot of movement and allowance is also made for a groin guard.

The top is usually a club T-shirt or jacket; the belt indicates the grade attained.

safety equipment

You will firstly need boxing gloves. Their weight may be 227 or 286g (8 or 10oz) for men, depending on the competition, but are always 286g (10oz) for women. Secondly, you will need padded footwear, and thirdly, a head guard, so that both your opponent and you are protected. Fourthly, boxing bandages will protect your hands and will give you a firm hold when you are wearing boxing gloves. The fifth, optional, requirement is shin guards, which will provide protection from impact when you are sparring or competing.

The mouth guard is a very important safety device that should be worn at all times when you are sparring and, of course, when you are competing in the ring. It is important to opt for a good-quality mouth guard. As a rough guide, the better and tighter the mouth guard fits, the more protection you will have. Note that you could buy a mouth guard that protects both your upper and lower jaw (when wearing it, you should clamp your teeth together and breathe through the integral breathing hole).

As its name suggests, a groin guard will protect your groin against any impact, particularly when high kicks are being performed, the groin being a target that can be unintentionally hit. The groin guard is a hard-plastic guard that has an elastic strip for a secure fit. It is worn under kickboxing trousers.

hand-wrapping

It is crucial to wrap your hands with boxing bandages because this will support your fingers and wrists, thus reducing the risk of injury. It also provides extra padding within your boxing gloves. When wrapping bandages around your hands, always start with your left hand and finish with your right hand.

There are different ways of wrapping your hands. Experiment to find the most comfortable for you.

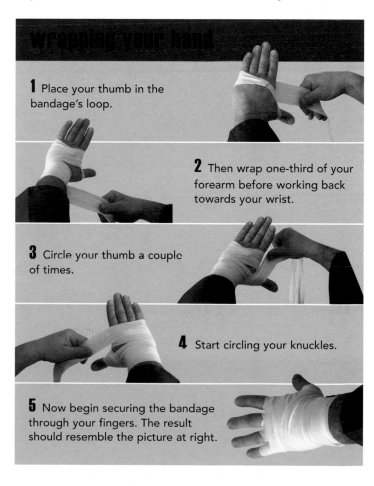

wrapping your hand

1 Place your thumb in the bandage's loop.

2 Then wrap one-third of your forearm before working back towards your wrist.

3 Circle your thumb a couple of times.

4 Start circling your knuckles.

5 Now begin securing the bandage through your fingers. The result should resemble the picture at right.

grading in kickboxing

Kickboxing has a similar grading system to that of any other martial art. However, the grading syllabus differs from organisation to organisation. There are usually eight belts before the black belt. Grading begins with the white belt, which indicates a novice. It then continues with the red, yellow, orange, green, blue, purple, brown, and finally, black belt, which it can take between three to four years to attain.

The grading syllabus normally consists of elements of fitness, kicks, punches, hand techniques, defence techniques, shadow sparring and sparring.

examples of a grading syllabus

The grading syllabus outlined below is typical for the yellow belt, but can, of course, vary from organisation to organisation.

fitness

Two minutes' skipping;
twenty press-ups;
twenty abdominal
    crunches;
twenty squat thrusts.

kicks

Five front kicks;
five roundhouse kicks;
five axe kicks.

punches

Five jabs;
five crosses;
five jab and crosses.

grade	
	white belt
	red belt
	yellow belt
	orange belt
	green belt
	blue belt
	purple belt
	brown belt
	black belt

grading for a black belt

A typical grading syllabus for a black belt is outlined below. As you will see, a person's physical fitness and fighting ability have to be very good in order to achieve a black belt.

fitness

Eight minutes' skipping;
sixty press-ups;
sixty abdominal crunches;
sixty squat thrusts.

kicks

(All of the kicks have to be performed for both sides.)
Five front kicks;
five side kicks;
five roundhouse kicks;
five axe kicks;
five turning back kicks;
five heel kicks;
five turning heel kicks;
five double roundhouse kicks with a step;
five heel kicks and roundhouse kicks with a step;
five double side kicks with a step;
five jumping front kicks;
five jumping roundhouse kicks;
five jumping, turning roundhouse kicks;
five jumping, turning back kicks;
five jumping, turning heel kicks.

punches and hand techniques

Five jabs;
five crosses;
five cross and hooks;
five jab, cross and jabs;
five jab and uppercuts
   performed with the same hand;
five double jab and crosses;
five jab, cross and hooks;
five retreating jabs;
five jab, slip and uppercuts;
five slip, hook and crosses;
five jab, cross, roll and hooks with the same hand;
five retreating jab and uppercuts;
five retreating jab and hooks with the same hand;

punches and hand techniques continued

five retreating jab, uppercut and hooks with the
   same hand;
five retreating jab, uppercut and hooks with the
   same hand and place a cross.

defence techniques

Sparring against given attacks.

sparring

Shadow sparring;
sparring.

training with equipment

No matter how skilled you are as a kickboxer, your training will include working with various pieces of equipment, such as focus mitts, focus paddles, Thai pads and kicking shields.

focus mitts

By using focus mitts, you will develop speed, power and timing, and will learn to aim at a specific target. When the mitts are moved into different positions, you will learn to react quickly and to adapt to a target. Above all, they will give you an excellent workout. With focus mitts, you can chose to place a punch or kick, and because they force you to focus on a very small striking area, they will increase your accuracy. The most important lesson to be learned is that of judging distance, in that you will begin to develop an instinctive feel for the distance to a target. You will also learn how to adjust your stance in order to place an effective kick or punch. Almost all kickboxing combinations can be practised with focus mitts.

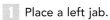

1 Place a left jab.

2 Follow up with a right cross.

3 Now direct a roundhouse kick at the head.

4 Then turn the focus mitt and place a turning hook kick.

the focus paddle

The focus paddle is an excellent training tool for improving your kicks. Its advantage is that as the target, it is somewhat removed from the body of the person holding it. You can therefore practise kicks that you would not normally attempt in case you hit him or her.

Other advantages are that you follow through and totally concentrate on your technique, and not on the power of the kick.

1 The first technique that can be practised with a focus paddle is a spinning hook kick.

2 Now try a spinning crescent kick.

3 Now try a roundhouse kick.

4 Without dropping the roundhouse kick, bring back your leg with a hook kick.

Thai pads

Because Thai pads are very well padded, they take the impact of a blow extremely effectively, giving the person holding them extra protection. They are also light, which means that they don't restrict your mobility. The versatility of Thai pads is demonstrated below.

1 In order to avoid injuring the person holding them, aim at the middle of the Thai pads.

2 Direct a roundhouse kick at the middle of the Thai pads.

3 Practise your knee strikes on Thai pads.

4 Work on your elbow strikes.

the kicking shield

When training, the kicking shield is a very useful piece of equipment for practising kicks. Because it is large, it gives the person holding it extra security. The kicks that are directed at a kicking shield include all kinds of side kicks, front kicks and roundhouse kicks.

1 Direct a side kick at the middle of the kicking shield.

2 The size of the kicking shield lessens the risk of injury to the person holding it.

3 Direct a front kick at the middle of the kicking shield.

4 Now try to deliver a spinning back kick to the middle of the kicking shield.

stances and footwork

It is vital to understand the importance of a stance and how to move out of it. Mastering this movement and preparing for the next kicking or boxing technique is crucial for any good fighter.

The stance is the foundation of all attacks and defences, and the more flowing your techniques, the faster you will be able to react and defend yourself, attack or counterattack.

It is vital to understand that all kicks and punches should be executed in a normal boxing stance. This stance allows you to perform any kick or punch, although you will probably have to make slight adjustments to your stance at times in order to deliver certain kicks. It is used in order to move into any technique without making your intentions obvious.

It is important to be light on your feet and to feel comfortable in your fighting stance. The famous phrase that the boxer Mohammed Ali used was: 'Float like a butterfly and sting like a bee'. When you watch footage of Ali, you soon realise how important footwork is. See the stance as the beginning of any technique in kickboxing. And the faster your footwork, the faster you will be in executing your techniques.

Because this squared-off position is so versatile, the fighting stance allows you maximum freedom of movement. It gives you a relatively low centre of gravity, enabling you to move from one side to another, as well as backwards and forwards.

fighting stance

The fighting stances for the right- and left-handed fighter are shown at right. The following explanation is for a right-handed fighter, but if you are left-handed, simply substitute 'left' for 'right' and so on.

Stand with your feet a shoulder-width apart, with your left foot about 60cm (2ft) in front of your right foot and both feet pointing slightly to the right. (Having your feet pointing to the right means that your body is turned to the side and presents your opponent with a reduced target area.) Ensure that your knees are slightly bent and keep your fists at chin level, with your lead hand a little extended. (This will enable you to protect your midsection at the same time as protecting your head with your fists.) Sixty per cent of your weight is on your front leg, but this can be adjusted, depending on the technique.

Fighting stance for the right-handed fighter.

Fighting stance for the left-handed fighter.

The traditional T-stance.

The T-stance seen from the side.

T-stance

When you compare the fighting stance with the T-stance that is used in more traditional martial arts, it becomes apparent that the weight distribution is different. In the T-stance, seventy per cent of your body weight is placed on your back leg, for example. It is an excellent stance if you are a good kicker and your kicking leg is in front of your body. However, this stance makes it hard to place a right cross without distributing your weight, and when you are distributing your weight, you are signalling to your opponent that you are about to place a punch. It is therefore important to learn to place any technique in the kickboxing fighting stance.

mobility

In kickboxing, good mobility and footwork are just as important as being able to kick and punch. Fighters who don't work on their footwork can look jerky and tense. The faster you are on your feet, the more graceful and quicker you will become. When your stance and footwork are good, you will also make better use of your body, in turn resulting in more powerful techniques.

Your ability to move from one position to another must become second nature because when you fight, you move either back and forth or from side to side at speed. Your balance and stability depend on you being able to maintain a good stance and sound footwork when you are moving quickly. If your stance is unstable, you will not have a good foundation on which to perform kickboxing movements and techniques. Not only will they lack power, but it will be hard for you to balance your body correctly if your stance is not right and your footwork lacks co-ordination. Able footwork and a good stance distinguish a good kickboxer from a less able one.

footwork

Working on their footwork is an exercise that is essential for kickboxing partners. When one partner is said to lead, this means that he or she goes forwards, backwards and sideways, with the other following. Not only are they practising their footwork, but working on their reactions and getting a feel for distance. Advanced kickboxers train in this way very quickly indeed.

Footwork is an extremely important factor when learning essential fighting techniques. Good footwork is vital if you are to attack and defend effectively because it determines your distance from your opponent. Footwork is always a starting point for any technique, for kicks and punches alike.

Footwork has to be mastered in order to ensure that you keep your balance in every possible situation. In order to achieve this, you have to practise it regularly so that every move becomes second nature. Even very experienced fighters practise their footwork over and over again, for every powerful punch or kick originates in good footwork.

Good footwork, coupled with a good stance, enables you to manoeuvre yourself into any position ready to kick, punch or block. Your opponent is not stationary, which means that you will have to learn to manage your space in order to be ready to take advantage of any opportunity. If your footwork is competent, you should be able to judge the correct distance to enable you accurately to place any technique that you wish to perform.

footwork when moving forwards

Your footwork will be displayed when you come out of a fighting stance. If you move forwards, you will move your leading leg first, and will drag your rear leg after it shortly afterwards. This move is called a 'step-drag'. When performing a step-drag, remember never to cross one foot over the other because this will prevent you from tripping over your feet.

1 The footwork is performed when coming out of a fighting stance

2 Move your front leg and position it in front of your body.

3 After you have positioned your front leg, drag your rear leg into position.

footwork when moving backwards

If you move backwards when coming out of a fighting stance, you will move your rear leg first and will drag your front leg after it shortly afterwards. This move is called a 'backwards step-drag'. When performing a backwards step-drag, do not cross your legs because you will lose your balance if you do so.

1 The footwork is performed when coming out of a fighting stance.

2 Move your back leg and position it behind your body.

3 After you have positioned your back leg, drag your front leg into position.

footwork when moving to the side

If you move sideways when coming out of a fighting stance, you will first move the leg that is closest to the side to which you want to move, and will then drag the leg that is further away towards it. When you perform this 'side-step-drag', do not cross your legs because this would put you off balance.

1 The footwork is performed when coming out of a fighting stance.

2 Move your left leg and position it to the left of your body.

3 After you have positioned your left leg, drag your right leg to the left, into position.

Follow steps 2 and 3, substituting 'right' for left' and 'left' for 'right', when moving to the right.

punches

Before we discuss boxing techniques, it is important to look at the basics and to stress the fact that repetition is the key to mastering a technique and then performing it to the best of your ability.

Even when you are an experienced fighter, you will find that continuing to work on the basics proves how important repetition is, for if you repeat a technique often enough, it will become second nature. It may be a long journey, but repetition will make you a good martial artist.

Until you master the basics, you will feel uncomfortable performing the more complex moves, and this will show in your technique. For instance, combinations will look rigid when you perform them, and a sequence will appear as though it consists of three or four movements put together rather than one, flowing movement.

Another point that it is important to accept is that boxing techniques are crucial in kickboxing. It often seems as though fighters who are good kickers feel that they can neglect their boxing techniques. The message is simple, however: be good at both kicking and boxing techniques, and you will be able to use more fighting strategies against different fighters. When you watch fights, you will soon realise that excellent kickers always use their kicking techniques to dominate a fight. Yet if you also have good boxing techniques, you can step into the kicker's range, work your punches and frustrate your opponent's fighting strategy.

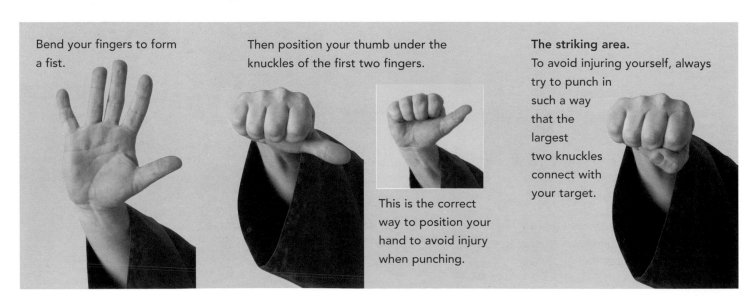

Bend your fingers to form a fist.

Then position your thumb under the knuckles of the first two fingers.

This is the correct way to position your hand to avoid injury when punching.

The striking area.
To avoid injuring yourself, always try to punch in such a way that the largest two knuckles connect with your target.

the jab

The jab is probably the most basic punch that you can learn in boxing. It is also the most important. It is not the most powerful, however, and should be practised in combination with other kicks and punches.

The jab can be used to keep an opponent away from you or to set you up to perform a follow-on technique. It can be used to test opponents, too, enabling you to see how they react, how they block and how fast they are. It can also be used to mislead and distract an opponent before you execute your own technique.

The jab can be used to deliver punches to the head or body, be it as a single punch or in rapid succession. You can use it to defend yourself from attack or as an attacking technique.

It is therefore important to learn how to throw a jab while you are moving backwards, forwards and sideways. Jab techniques can be used with a step in order to throw your body weight behind the punch, but they can also be performed from a stationary position when an opponent is within your reach or stepping into your space.

1 Start in a fighting stance, with both hands raised to protect your body. Your lead, or right, hand should be in front of your body, and your left hand should be protecting your face.

2 When you jab, turn your fist so that your palm is facing downwards. This will add a whip-like effect to your movement. Remember to turn your body into the punch.

3 When you place the punch and your fist is fully turned, it is important to think about defence. It should therefore be as though your left hand is glued to your face, while your jaw is protected by your shoulder (note that you should tuck your chin behind your shoulder).

4 Pull back your fist and assume a fighting stance, with your fists and arms protecting your face and body.

the right cross

The right cross, which is also referred to as the 'straight right', is a very powerful punch that can achieve a lot of knockouts. Like the jab, it can be directed at the head or body.

The right cross can be used as an attacking, defending or counterattacking technique. It is very powerful as a counterattacking technique because when opponents attack you, they bring their body weight forward, so that when you punch, the combination of your opponent's body weight and your own will help you to land a very powerful punch, to devastating effect.

When executing this punch, it is important to throw your body weight into it, which means that you will have to pivot on your rear leg in order to obtain a better reach and add power to your punch.

1 Begin in a fighting stance, with your lead hand in front of your body and your right hand at the side of your face.

2 Turn your fist so that your palm is facing downwards. Turn your body into the punch.

3 As you fully extend your arm and place the punch, make sure that your chin is tucked behind your shoulder to protect it from any blows. Pivot on your rear leg in order to put your body weight behind the punch. Snap back your fist and assume a fighting stance.

the hook

The hook is a very effective technique that results in more knockouts than any other punch. This is because you throw your body weight behind it. It can be directed at the head or body, depending on the situation in which you find yourself and the targets that are open to you.

Rather than moving straight forward, when executing the hook, your body makes a rotating twist on its own axis in order to generate power. Your front leg pivots on its foot, bringing your body weight forward, and you should also rotate your shoulder and hip. It is important to throw your whole body weight into the hook and then to follow through in order to give your punch speed and power.

1 Assume a fighting stance.

2 Now turn your fist so that your palm is facing downwards.

3 When executing the hook, your body should make a rotating twist and your arm should be moving in an arc parallel to the ground. Pivot on your front foot and throw your body weight behind the punch. Then snap back your fist and assume a fighting stance, with your guard up in order to protect your body and face.

the uppercut

When you watch kickboxing fights, it becomes apparent that many fighters neglect the uppercut. When performed well, however, it can be a nasty punch that can result in a knockout. It is only when some fighters are at the receiving end of an uppercut that they realise that it is a very effective weapon to include in their fighting arsenal.

The uppercut can be classified as a close-range punch that travels directly upwards to connect with an opponent's chin, floating ribs or solar plexus.

The uppercut's power is generated by turning the shoulders and hips and by bending the knees and then straightening them before impact. If this sequence is performed seamlessly, the punch will have a tremendous impact. Although it can be executed with your lead (left) or right hand, a right-hand uppercut will always generate more power than a lead- or left-hand uppercut.

1 Assume a fighting stance.

2 Turn your fist so that your palm is facing towards you. Turn slightly to the right and bend your knees.

3 Now generate maximum power by straightening your knees and turning your shoulders and hips to produce an upward surge with your whole body. Then snap back your fist and return to the fighting stance. Due to the nature of the punch, you remain very near to your opponent and may consequently now wish to use other kicking or punching combinations.

the back-fist strike

The back-fist strike is a fast strike that can be used to distract or disorientate an opponent. It is not a very powerful punch, but it can set you up to use any kicking or punching combination, such as a kick or a powerful right.

When executing a back-fist strike, aim at the side of the head, which you should hit with your knuckles.

1 Assume a fighting stance, with your lead hand in front of your body and your right hand by the side of your face.

2 Pull back your lead hand and body before striking. Your lead hand should move across your face.

3 Place your back-fist strike so that your knuckles connect with the side of your opponent's head. Remember to follow through with your whole body.

You could follow this strike with a boxing combination, but if you don't, make sure that you raise your guard when resuming a fighting stance.

kicks

As its name suggests, kickboxing includes a variety of kicks. These are similar to the kicks that are performed in other martial arts, but tend to be those that are the most effective in the ring.

Before we discuss any kicks, it is important that you are familiar with the foot's various striking areas. These are: the ball of the foot (1); the top of the foot (2); the sole of the foot (3); the foot's inside edge (4); the foot's outside edge (5); the bottom of the heel (6); and the back of the heel (7). (See also the box below.)

Remember that it is important to position your toes and foot properly, as well as to use the correct striking area, if you are to execute a good kick and minimise the risk of injuring yourself.

Kickboxing uses kicks as its bread-and-butter techniques because of the power and range that they give a fighter.

Kicks are therefore seen as being an important part of a

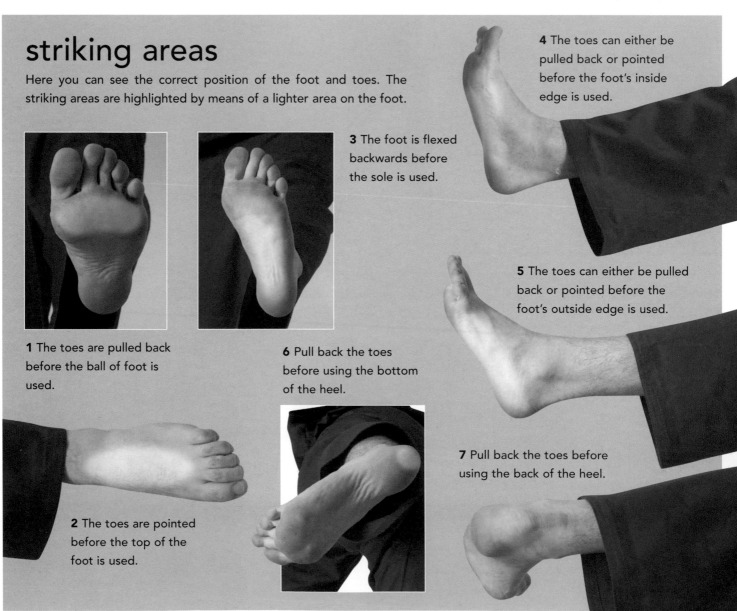

striking areas

Here you can see the correct position of the foot and toes. The striking areas are highlighted by means of a lighter area on the foot.

3 The foot is flexed backwards before the sole is used.

4 The toes can either be pulled back or pointed before the foot's inside edge is used.

1 The toes are pulled back before the ball of foot is used.

6 Pull back the toes before using the bottom of the heel.

5 The toes can either be pulled back or pointed before the foot's outside edge is used.

2 The toes are pointed before the top of the foot is used.

7 Pull back the toes before using the back of the heel.

kickboxer's success, and intensively practising their movements, speed and power will always result in both graceful and explosive techniques.

Although kicks are the hardest element of this martial art to learn and master, doing so is not only most satisfying, but makes the difference between a good and a very good kickboxer.

It is important to understand that the whole body is involved in a kick, not just the leg and foot. To make the kick more effective, your body can move either towards or away from the target, depending on the kick that you are performing. It is the motion of your body that gives you an extra surge of power.

Another crucial point to appreciate is that your hips should turn with the kick, thereby maximising its power because you are injecting the force of your body weight into the technique. Using your hips will give you greater reach, too, because you hold your body far looser, enabling you to reach higher when kicking.

It is also vital to understand the importance of positioning your foot correctly when placing a kick. In order to obtain the best position for most of the kicks, you should direct the heel of the pivoting foot on the ground at the target. (This is less commonly done for a front kick, however.)

Once you have mastered the kicking techniques outlined in this chapter, they will be among your most powerful tools. If your kicks are powerful and fast, and you have good control over them, your opponent will have difficulty influencing the fight.

Kicks can be executed just as quickly as punches, but from further away, and the feet are also more resilient than the hands. You can generate three times as much power with a kick tha n you can with a punch, but this power can only be released when the correct techniques are used. (More energy is required to perform a kick than a punch, however, while athletes with long legs will have a major advantage over opponents with shorter legs.)

These are just some of the reasons why kickboxers spend so much time focusing on improving their kicks. Kicking is also an excellent cardiovascular workout. In addition, learning defensive and offensive kicking techniques, as well as the necessary footwork and body movements, requires you to use all of the major muscle groups simultaneously.

Every time that a kick is performed, the front and side abdominal, or stomach, muscles are used to raise the leg in readiness for that kick. Kicking will therefore tone and strengthen your abdominal muscles in particular, thereby protecting you from injuries and helping you to endure kicks and blows to your body. Having strong abdominal muscles will allow you to twist your body more, too. And because the abdominal muscles connect your upper body to your lower body, if they are strong, they will help you to produce a more dynamic kick.

If you are to perform them well, and to merge them effectively later, it is vital that you understand the differences between the various kicks, as outlined on the following pages.

the front kick

The front kick is the first to be learned in most martial arts because it is simple and fast. When performed well, it can be used in tournament fighting and sparring. You can perform it with your front or back foot as an advancing or stopping technique. It can be a snap or push kick.

the front snap kick

To perform a front snap kick, raise your kicking leg in front of you and chamber it towards your target, so that you raise and bend your knee. The striking area for this kick is the ball of the foot, which is why you should pull back your toes and aim your foot at your target before snapping it out towards him or her.

To make it more powerful, it is important to remember to lean towards your target when performing the front snap kick.

This kick can also be executed with the front leg, in which case you would have to move back onto your rear, supporting leg and push yourself forwards with it.

1 Assume a fighting stance, with your fists raised to protect your body and head.

2 Raise and bend your knee into the chamber position. Ensure that your foot is pointing at your target.

3 Pull back your toes. Pivot on your supporting leg to enable your other hip to whip around and the ball of your foot to make contact with your target.

4 Snap back your foot into the chamber position and pivot back around on your supporting leg.

5 Position your kicking leg either in front of your body or behind it, in the starting position, whichever you prefer.

the front push kick

The front push kick can be seen as an offensive or defensive kick, depending on how it is executed. When the front leg is raised and pushed towards the opponent, it can be used a defence. When a strike is made with the sole of the foot, it can be used to fend off attackers. This technique is very useful because it enables you to give your opponent a big push, thereby throwing him or her off balance after blocking an attack. This push can provide you with sufficient distance in which to attack or counterattack by aiming follow-up kicks at your opponent.

The front push kick can be performed with the front or rear leg. It is important that you lean forward into the kick and raise your knee as high as possible before placing the kick.

The striking area is the sole of the foot. In order to avoid injuring yourself, pull back your toes and flex your foot before kicking out.

To make it more powerful, it is important to remember to lean towards your target when performing the front push kick.

This kick can also be executed with the front leg, in which case you would have to move back onto your rear, supporting leg and push yourself forwards with it.

1 Assume a fighting stance, with your fists raised to protect your body and head.

2 Pull your attacking leg up, towards your chest, ensuring that your knee is fully bent, your toes are pulled back and your foot is flexed.

3 Kick out with the sole of your flexed foot. When placing the kick, lean into it and pivot on your supporting leg to enable you to use your hip.

4 Snap your foot back into the starting position and pivot back on your supporting leg.

5 Position your kicking leg either in front of your body or behind it, whichever you prefer.

the roundhouse kick

The roundhouse kick is probably the most frequently used kick in sparring and competition fighting. When you watch competition fighting, it becomes apparent that the roundhouse kick is used on average four times as often as any other. It is therefore a very important kick to master.

Often used to attack or counterattack, this kick is very versatile and can easily be used in combination with other kicks and hand techniques. It is a very fast and powerful kick that can deliver a powerful blow to the side of an opponent's head or body.

It is important to lean into the roundhouse kick in order to move forwards. This kick can also be used defensively, when you will move backwards .

The striking area is the top of the foot, which should be pointed at the target to facilitate its placement at the side of the head or body.

Before placing the kick, your lower leg should be moving parallel to the ground. When placing the kick, lean into it and pivot on your supporting leg. The heel of your supporting foot should be pointing at the target before turning your foot 180 degrees.

1 Assume a fighting stance, with your fists raised to protect your body and head.

2 Point your toes, bend your knee and push your kicking leg back, towards your target.

3 Keep your toes pointing at your target before the top of your foot connects with it.

4 Snap your foot back into the starting position.

5 Position your kicking leg either in front of your body or behind it, whichever you prefer.

the side kick

The side kick is renowned for its graceful appearance and powerful impact. It is one of the hardest basic kicks to learn, but is a very useful technique to have in your competition arsenal.

The side kick can be executed with the front or back leg and serves as an attacking or defensive technique. Fighters with long legs tend to rely on it as a front-leg technique to be used as a defensive technique against an attacker.

The front-leg side kick does not differ greatly from the rear-leg side kick; it is just a question of where to balance your body weight. Which kick you use will be determined by the distance between you and your opponent. To perform the perfect side kick, it is important to align your ankle, knee, hip and shoulder in a straight line, and not to let your shoulder move out of alignment.

The striking areas are the heel or outside edge of the foot. To avoid injuring yourself, pull back your toes and flex your foot.

This very useful technique can be quick and effective when used in a variety of combinations.

1 Assume a fighting stance, with your fists raised to protect your body and head.

2 Bend your knee as you pull your kicking leg towards your chest, with your heel pointing at your target. It is important to chamber your leg as high as possible and to pivot on your supporting leg through 180 degrees so that your heel is pointing at the target.

3 When placing the kick, remember to direct your foot's striking area at the target. Your foot and leg should not dip or curve, but should travel in a straight line. Your foot should be flexed on impact, and your toes should be pointing downwards so that you can twist your hip into the target.

4 Position your kicking foot either in front of your body or behind it as you assume a fighting stance again.

the back kick

The back kick is a favourite weapon in many a kickboxer's arsenal because of the power that it can generate. As well as being powerful (and it is not uncommon to see it delivering a knockout blow to the body), it can be performed very quickly. This kick is so powerful partly because the gluteus maximus, the largest muscle in the body, is used to execute it and partly because of the energy that is produced when turning into it.

The back kick can be used as an attacking or counterattacking technique. When it is used as a retreating technique and the kicker is moving backwards, it still unleashes great power. And when the fighter is counterattacking, the back kick does not offer an opponent any targets, which is why it is valued as a safe kick.

The striking area is the heel. Before executing this kick, pull back your toes and flex your foot to avoid injuring yourself.

1 Assume a fighting stance, with your fists raised to protect your body and head. In order to place a back kick, it is important to turn your supporting foot through 180 degrees towards your target. Your head should be turning on the same side as your kicking leg and your shoulder should be pointing towards your opponent. Never lose sight of your target.

2 With your weight on your supporting leg, move your kicking leg forward from the rear. The back kick is different to the side kick in that the knee is not lifted, but instead stays low and close to the supporting leg.

3 Execute the back kick by kicking your kicking leg straight behind your supporting leg. Your foot should travel from the ground to your target. Depending on the situation, you should then place your foot either in front of you or, if you are retreating, behind you.

jumping kicks

Mention jumping kicks, and many people will visualise beautiful kicks forcing their way through the air to head height. Indeed, when jumping kicks are performed by a good martial artist, they are so good to watch that they invariably attract the attention of an audience. But unless a kickboxer has specialised in the technique and can execute it quickly, relatively few high, standard, jumping kicks are performed in the kickboxing ring.

Almost any kick that we have discussed so far can be performed as a jumping kick, giving you a lot of scope. But note that once you are in the air, it is difficult to change direction to perform another attacking or defensive kick. Remember that you are faster on the ground.

There are too many ways of preparing to perform jumping kicks for them all to be included here, so we will instead focus on one of the main jumping kicks: the jumping front kick.

the jumping front kick

There are different ways of preparing to perform a jumping front kick, depending on what you want the kick to achieve and how high you want to place it. It is important to remember that everybody has a different, and preferred, way of placing this kick.

The jumping front kick can be used as either an attacking or a defending technique. It can enable you to gain extra ground in order to move forwards and incorporate this technique into your attacking strategy or to get out of a situation that you are not controlling.

A traditional method of learning this kick appears here. Once you have mastered this technique, you can use the jumping front kick when you are moving backwards or forwards, and even when you are standing still.

The striking area is the ball or sole of the foot. Remember to pull back your toes and to ensure that your foot is pointing towards the target.

1 Assume a fighting stance, with your fists raised to protect your body and head.

2 Pull your non-kicking leg in a chambering position as high as you can towards your chest in order to gain height.

3 Then chamber your kicking leg just before it reaches the highest point.

4 Execute a front kick as though your foot were still on the ground. Pull your non-kicking leg towards your body and raise your fists to protect youself against any counterattack.

5 After you have perfomed the kick, snap back your leg and then land in a forward fighting stance.

low kicks and sweeps

There are two main low kicks: one directed at the outside of the thigh and the other, to the inside of the thigh. Both are similar to the roundhouse kick, except that the striking area is the shin.

Low kicks and sweeps are techniques that can be used to add variety to fighting styles and strategies. They are used in both kickboxing and Thai-boxing contests, although low kicks are not performed in full-contact fights in which all of the kicks are placed above the waist.

low kicks

Low kicks are effective techniques that can cause knockouts. Indeed, they can be so devastating that they make excellent self-defence applications.

1 An inside low kick being directed at the front of an opponent's inner thigh. The fighter doing the kicking uses his hip to whip his leg towards his opponent.

2 The outside low kick is similar to the inside low kick, except that the fighter doing the kicking aims for the outside of his opponent's thigh.

Note that these kicks are placed with the shin.

sweeping an opponent

The aim of the sweeping technique is to sweep your opponent off balance, or even to throw him or her to the floor. When your opponent is off balance, he or she will find it difficult to mount a defence against any further attack that you may be planning.

Before sweeping your opponent, remember that most of your weight should be on your sweeping leg.

strikes

The strikes discussed in this chapter can be performed with the knee or elbow. They are excellent close-quarter techniques that can be used very effectively in self-defence situations.

knee strikes

Knee strikes are simple, but effective, techniques that can have a devastating effect if executed correctly. Indeed, the knees are not commonly used in fights precisely because of the damage that they can cause. It is nevertheless important to grasp how knee strikes are performed because they are such effective applications when it comes to self-defence.

The knee strike can be aimed at the torso or the thigh, whose muscles may go into spasm and be afflicted by cramp when hit.

elbow strikes

Elbow strikes are mainly used in Thai boxing and muay thai. Very powerful and dangerous techniques, the striking area is the elbow, which means that you are driving a pointed, hard bone towards your opponent. Elbow strikes are excellent attacking and defensive techniques that can be made at close range. When executing an elbow strike, remember that it is important to rotate your hips and shoulders in order to maximise the strike's power.

the front knee strike

The front knee strike is performed with your rear leg. Although the initial stages resemble those of a front kick, at the point that you would place the front kick, you leave your knee in the chambering position and drive it forwards, rather than upwards, into the opponent's body or thigh. When you pull your opponent downwards, you will also have an opportunity to strike his or her head.

1 It is important to keep your guard up when your attacker comes forward.

2 Chamber your rear leg and grasp your opponent as you bring your leg forward.

3 When you execute the strike, make sure that you direct the force forwards, not upwards.

the outside knee strike

As its name suggests, the outside knee strike is executed from the outside of your body, the aim being to strike your opponent's floating ribs or thigh. The effectiveness of this technique is particularly evident if you watch muay thai matches, when you will see fighters getting their opponents in headlocks before executing the strike with either their rear or front legs.

1 Assume a fighting stance before executing an outside knee strike.

2 After grabbing your opponent's neck, lift your rear leg into a chambering position.

3 Pull your opponent towards you and then bring in your knee, aiming at the ribcage.

the front elbow strike

The front elbow strike follows a circular path towards the side of an opponent's head. The body movement is similar to that of a hook, and it is important to turn your body into the strike.

1 If the distance between you and your opponent allows it, you can execute a front elbow strike in a fighting stance.

2 A close-quarter technique, the front elbow strike travels in a horizontal manner. Turn your whole body into the strike, pivoting on your front leg if necessary.

3 It is important to remember to allow your hips and rear leg to turn, too, in order to generate power. This strike can be placed with either the rear or lead hand.

the upward elbow strike

The upward elbow strike resembles an uppercut, but instead of hitting your opponent with your fist, you use your elbow bone to strike his or her chin. This is an excellent way of getting past an opponent's defences.

1 Prepare to push past your opponent's defences by assuming a fighting stance.

2 The upward elbow strike can be performed with either your rear or lead hand, travelling vertically.

3 To gain extra power, use your leg to catapult you into making the upward elbow strike.

blocking

When kickboxers cannot avoid blows being made against their bodies, they will try to block those blows in order to prevent any real damage from being inflicted on them.

blocking and avoiding punches

Avoiding blows being made to your head or body is part of your defence. Whatever you do that prevents an opponent from landing blows on your head or body is classified as a defensive move.

You can defend your body by parrying (redirecting a punch) or by blocking an attack, by slipping, by bobbing and weaving or by moving out of the way by side-stepping or by feinting.

Note that if it is to absorb the impact of a punch, a block has to be made as close to your body as possible.

parrying

Parrying is a simple, but effective, way of redirecting a punch. It is normally used against a jab or right cross directed at your head. Parry with your lead hand, using only minimal movements, in order to redirect the force of the punch, which should miss your head by a small margin. The more you minimise your movements, the quicker you can return to the on-guard position.

1 Prepare to parry a jab in the fighting stance by unclenching your hand inside your boxing glove. When deflecting the jab with your hand, remember that minimising the move will enable you to counter your opponent's attack with a kick or a punch.

2 Prepare to parry a right cross in the fighting stance by first unclenching your hand inside your boxing glove. When deflecting the right cross with your hand, minimise the move in order to counterattack with a kick or a punch.

blocking

Blocking is a key skill that is very effective when you are not able to get away from a blow or are not fast enough to parry it. If you want to avoid receiving the blow, you will have to block it.

When you have practised these techniques often enough, you will automatically begin to know when to parry and when to block.

blocking punches to the body

1 When blocking a jab to your body, turn your body and then take the jab with your forearm or elbow.

2 When blocking a right cross, turn your body and then take the right cross with your forearm or elbow.

This technique can be used to block any punch directed at the body, which is why it is important to practise different variations of this defensive block.

blocking punches to the head

Punches to the head are blocked with the elbow or forearm. While you are blocking a punch, continue to move away from your opponent's fist in order to deflect the impact of the punch.

When blocking a blow to the head, it is vital that you protect yourself by holding your elbows and arms tightly against your body. As your opponent's fist comes towards you, tuck your chin down, onto your chest, turn away your face slightly and try to let your glove take the impact of the punch.

blocking an uppercut

When blocking an uppercut directed at your chin, your technique should have elements of a parry and elements of a block. Which hand you use depends on the hand that your opponent is using to make the uppercut. Unclench your fingers inside your glove and block the punch as through you were parrying it, thereby stopping the uppercut's upward motion.

the bob and weave

The bob and weave is used both to evade swinging punches aimed at your head and to create a moving target so that your opponent will find it difficult to aim for, and hit, your head. Move in a circular direction while shifting your head clear of the punch.

1 While weaving, drop your body by bending your legs.

2 Your opponent's punch now whistles past your head.

3 Move to the other side and come back up again with your guard in place. You are now in an excellent position to counterattack.

blocking and avoiding kicks

When you are defending your body against kicks, it is vital that you appreciate how powerful they can be. One thing that sets kickboxing apart from other competitive martial arts is that kicks can be directed towards an opponent's legs, which is why it is important to learn how to block them. Although you should learn how to avoid and block kicks, you will not always be able to fend off contact, which is why we will also cover redirecting kicks.

blocking with the shin

Blocking with the shin is a very effective way of blocking a blow aimed at the thigh or calf. Imagine that you are the fighter pictured on the right in the photographs below, blocking the attack.

1 You are standing in a fighting stance when your opponent tries to direct a turning kick at your outer leg.

2 You shift your weight on to your back leg before raising your front leg and turning your body through 45 degrees so that your shin blocks your opponent's kick.

redirecting kicks

Redirecting a kick is a technique that is used to evade a front kick, a very powerful kick that is generally aimed at the middle of the body. By redirecting the kick, you will effectively avoid receiving the full force of its impact, but will still be close enough to counterattack.

Use your left hand to redirect a front kick that your opponent is executing with his or her left leg. Make sure that you shift your body out of the way by moving your hips backwards and taking a small step to the opposite side of your opponent's kicking leg. This means that when your opponent kicks with his or her left leg, you take a small step to the right, and when the kick is made with the right leg, you take a small step to the left.

If your opponent kicks with his or her rear leg, step backwards before redirecting it.

1 A redirection is performed in the fighting stance. When redirecting a kick from your opponent's left leg, make sure that you move your body out of the path of the kick by taking a small step to the right. Also remember to pull your hips back.

2 Taking a step to the right ensures that you are safely out of the kick's path in case you don't catch your opponent's leg. Simultaneously block the kick and redirect it with the inner side of your boxing glove.

getting out of a headlock

When you find yourself in a headlock, it is important to get out of this vulnerable position as soon as possible before your opponent decides to bombard you with a hail of devastating knee strikes. One way of doing this is to counterattack with a headlock of your own.

1 The headlock is a strong hold. Try to create space between you and your opponent by pushing his or her head to the side. Do this by moving your left arm over your opponent's arms.

2 Your opponent's grip will slacken, creating a gap in his or her hold. Slide your right hand through the gap and grab your opponent's neck.

3 Now slip your left hand through the same gap.

You have now released **4** your opponent's grip and can hold him or her in a headlock. You have the upper hand and can decide what to do next.

conclusion

As you will have learned, there are similarities and differences between the different martial arts discussed in this book. the guides to the techniques have provided a good overview of what to expect if you decide to go to a class, or learn more about one or more of the disciplines.

Maybe you have already decided which martial art you prefer, or which you feel most suited to. If so your next step should be to find out about classes in your area - there are usually many different classes and styles available. If you are still undecided, then why not try each of them? Most classes will offer a free tester session, where you will get a better idea of what approach works best for you.

We hope you have enjoyed this book, and have gained enjoyment, as well as a better understanding of the principles and philosophies - not to mention the techniques - of each of the six disciplines described.

When you have found the style that is yours, nothing can stop you from training. It will become an integral part of your lifestyle. Motivating yourself to train is no longer the issue. It is more likely that you will find difficulty with not training. Good luck in your Martial Arts journey.

Choosing a style

So how do you choose the correct martial arts' style for yourself? Once you have decided that you would like to try to learn a martial art, how do you stop yourself from choosing the wrong path; especially with modern day advertising, which tries to attract students to a particular school of training?

The answer is simple. Pick a style that you like the look of and give it a try. Part of martial arts' training is having the courage to act on your own instincts. If it looks good to you, try it. The most difficult step to make is the first one. Once you have tried, many of the mental barriers that you thought existed will simply dissolve. A commonly quoted phrase in martial arts is that ' A journey of ten thousand miles has to start with the first step'.

If you stay concious of what you are doing and follow your own inner self (another martial arts' skill), then it will not matter if you chop and change through several styles. This simply means that you are still trying to find the style that suits you the most. This part of the learning may take quite some time, but there can be many valuable lessons to be gained from it.

index

further reading

The Judo Handbook, Roy Inman, 2004

The Karate Handbook, Ray Pawlett, 2004

The Tae Kwon Do Handbook, Mark and Ray Pawlett, 2004

The Kickboxing Handbook, Mark Ritschel, 2004

The Kung Fu Handbook, Peter Warr, 2004

The Ju Jitsu Handbook, Roy Inman, 2004

credits and acknowledgements

The publishers would like to thank the authors whose knowledge, experience and expertise have contributed to making this an excellent guide to martial arts techniques.

We would also like to thank the martial arts practitioners who demonstrate their skills in this book. These are as follows:

Karate: John Hurley, Glenn Stevens, Sam Wright.

Judo: Michelle Holt, Jason Parsons, Tom Reed.

Tae Kwon Do: Master Foran, Mrs Foran, Mr Tully.

Kung Fu: Peter Warr, Edward Gomersall, Elaine Koster.

Ju Jitsu: Andy Burns, Michelle Holt, Sian Wilson.

Kickboxing: John Ritschel, Dave Gentry, Leanne Phillips, Mark Blundell